W9-BME-256

MAP

Urban Gathering: A Fable

Often, beginnings are a path into the development of an idea, an invention, even the seed of a tree. At the beginning is clarity, one can see the end. At the beginning of the human life, in the mother's womb, is the story of its eventuality, not only of birth but the genomic makeup of a human being that is born and lives a life.

It's going back to those beginnings in medicine that they are now trying to find clarity and sometimes alterations to make life longer and more pleasant and more healthy.

I have thought of that moment when disparate individuals symbolically sat in a circle around the fire for warmth, for cooking, for companionship in the very beginnings of our pre-history, who in some manner with sign language, grunts and sounds, had the realization that each individual around that circle appeared to do something better than the others.

With the then recently discovered **fire** is an individual who understands a spark, the heating of wood against wood, the making of the fire. Another seems to be better in moving place to place in keeping that fire alive. Someone can discover **flint** from other stones or **obsidian**, and that person figures out how to flake off the edges, an extremely difficult task even now, perhaps 350,000 years later. These can be used as knives for skinning creatures or strapped to the end of a piece of wood as an arrow or spear. Someone else can throw the spear. There's the obvious distinction of which sex gives birth and provides the original sustenance for the newborn.

By trial and error and memory, the poison berries and the poison mushrooms are not eaten, and those that provide food can be gathered by someone with that knowledge. Some people are just better at that than others.

This is a very special moment, the understanding, the realization of this. The realization that everybody doesn't do everything is the beginning of a group made up of a family or 2 that are naturally composed, particularly with the birth of a child, and these groups become a tribe, a village, a town and then a city.

A city is a place where clearly everybody doesn't do everything. It's where we are today. I don't know where we'll be tomorrow.

FIRE
The earliest evidence for fire associated with humans comes from Oldowan hominid sites in the Lake Turkana region of Kenya. The site known as Koobi Fora contained oxidized patches of earth to a depth of several centimeters, which some scholars interpret as evidence for fire control. At 1.4 million years of age, the Australopithecine site of Chesowanja in central Kenya also contained burned clay clasts, in small areas.

FLINT
Flint has been used by humans to make stone tools for at least 2 million years. The conchoidal fracture of flint causes it to break into sharp-edged pieces. Early people recognized this property of flint and learned how to fashion it into knife blades, spear points, arrowheads, scrapers, axes, drills and other sharp tools using a method known as flint knapping. If these tools were broken or damaged in use they were often reshaped into smaller tools of similar function.

OBSIDIAN
Obsidian is a naturally occurring volcanic glass formed as an extrusive igneous rock. It is produced when felsic lava extruded from a volcano cools rapidly with minimal crystal growth. Obsidian is commonly found within the margins of rhyolitic lava flows known as obsidian flows, where the chemical composition (high silica content) induces a high viscosity and polymerization degree of the lava. The inhibition of atomic diffusion through this highly viscous and polymerized lava explains the lack of crystal growth. Obsidian is hard and brittle; it therefore fractures with very sharp edges, which were used in the past in cutting and piercing tools, and it has been used experimentally as surgical scalpel blades.

The ability, the natural inclination to specialize, is both our strength and our weakness. It's weak because we end up in the narrowing of our lives and our ability to survive difficult situations and a lack of appreciation for the complexity of life. But as you specialize, it gives people the ability to get deeper and deeper into a subject and take the investigation of that subject further.

That's been one of the battles in our learning system of whether to be well-rounded or a specialist. It also determines how you live your life and what your interests are, and whether you miss the opportunities of new ideas through the convergence of varying ideas from different specialties and discover things that wouldn't be discovered otherwise.

It's a fundamental conflict and very clear in our society today as it was when they sat around the fire and made this amazing leap that only humans seem to have done, of desiring to remember and record what they learned and experienced. To keep the story alive, which they did through gestures, grunts to words, words to music and pictures on walls, walls that today seem perhaps even more magical than when they were initially created. The mystery increases their beauty and the essence of the event they recorded under the worst lighting conditions and was obviously the invention, the discovery of something that had colors and apparently would last.

Think about doing that today. Few of us could make a fire, or find a piece of flint and make a flinthead. Many archeologists have experimented with doing it and eventually learned how, but it's very difficult, it's not an easy task, it's one of the more difficult badges to attain in scouting, and few of us can do it.

Nor could the Picasso's in our midst draw as incisively or beautifully, and perhaps none of us could do it in the dark, damp cold of a **cave**, and have it last for 35,000 years.This comes from the early specialties of the earliest of man. It's really quite a beautiful story that Hollywood has not given its due. That the beginnings of things are magnitudes harder to identify and embrace and are often thrown aside in our desire to learn the exquisiteness of the sophistications of history, painting, writing and music.

In the beginning of one of my books, and I've said it other times in this book, is a quote that touches the depth of my days. It is a quote from Lou Kahn, and it is quite simply *Beginnings, beginnings, I love beginnings.* Lou saw that in the beginning was the possibility of the end and in the seed was the flower and I find that an exciting way to start each idea.

MESOPOTAMIA
The ancient city-states of Mesopotamia in an area known as the fertile crescent are most cited by Western and Middle Eastern scholars as the cradle of civilization. The convergence of the Tigris and Euphrates Rivers produced rich fertile soil and a supply of water for irrigation. The civilizations that emerged around these rivers are among the earliest known non-nomadic agrarian societies. Because Ubaid, Sumer, Akkad, Assyria and Babylon all emerged around the Tigris-Euphrates, the theory that Mesopotamia is the cradle of civilization has enjoyed some credence.

3

FROM HAND TO MOUTH
In his book, *From Hand to Mouth: The Origins of Language*, Michael Corballis said: "Language developed much more gradually, starting with the gestures of apes, then gathering momentum as the bipedal hominids evolved. The appearance of the larger-brained genus Homo some 2 million years ago may have signaled the emergence and later development of syntax, with vocalizations providing a mounting refrain. What may have distinguished Homo sapiens was the final switch from a mixture of gestural and vocal communication to an autonomous vocal language, embellished by gesture but not dependent on it.

We walk in our cities and see garbage and think of more garbage cans.

We design light poles not lighting.

We own one half of the land in our cities and our concern is only with the look of the other half. We have an obsessive concern for plots of ownership and the building of private objects.

We think of solutions in terms of products not performance.

We ask for parks not places of recreation.

We value stylish graphics not communication.

We anguish over more school facilities and ignore the unlimited classroom that is our city.

We worry over disorientation and the anxiety about urban problems without allowing the city itself to become observable and understandable.

We don't even allow our children to comprehend the elements that make up, effect and allow for change in our human-made environment.

We are in a human-made forest – and it is as if the trees were falling and we could not see or hear them.

MAP
Mankind's Ability to Perceive

CITY/2

1/2 THE CITY BELONGS TO YOU
An Exhibition for the Philadelphia Museum of Art
June 1970

Perhaps it appears that I'm a contrarian ... actually I beleive everybody else.

CITY/2 is a fraction.

CITY/2 is the title of these comments

CITY/2 is the half of the city that the city and therefore its citizens own - ground floor of public buildings, parks, schools, streets, sidewalks and the space between things.

CITY/2 is what we own.

Architects, planners, cartographers, graphic designers and product designers have been participants in an endless marathon beautifying the physical form of our cities piece by piece, pitting one extruded building against another – seeking praise for high styled packages that misrepresent their contents and ignore their neighbors. Bling's the thing in architecture.

Designers have become urban Elizabeth Arden's applying mascara and calling it beautification and promoting urban Edsel's and calling them street furniture.

We have ignored the responsibility that the private environment has to the public environment and have not understood it as a major determinant of physical space.

Our magazines and museums promote the development of temporal tastes, creating showplaces for the product beautiful and publications for the building of the month.

Emphasis on the building's performance is considered secondary to the building's style.

Our comprehensive plans habitually segment our land and we apply zoning on a patchwork system of artificial verticality, whereas our cities actually demand the absolute opposite approach.

Our collective life style relates to horizontal layers of uses not vertical ones.

The most critical of these layers is the entire ground floor of the city.

A ground floor that should be publicly oriented and publicly owned or controlled, and should offer the invitation for:

UNDERSTANDING
LEARNING - the city as a schoolhouse.
SHOPPING
ORIENTATION
SAFETY
MOVEMENT
RECREATION
AND PERFORMANCES OF ALL KINDS

The public environment is another way of labeling the City/2 and the commonality of its spaces.

Taken as a whole, the public environment is the largest single use of land in the average American city, on average 50% and above. It is all the land that the city itself owns and controls. It is the sidewalks and streets it is the space between private buildings. It is where all mass transportation occurs. It is from where all shopping initiates. It is the place in which all communication about the city is transferred and all goods move. It is all the places and spaces that all the citizens use. It creates the major image of the city to the visitor and it is the measure of the life of a city at daytime or nighttime. This is true globally and can be mapped. The ground floor of public buildings, parks, etc. In order to establish the potential resource of the public environment we should ascertain certain performance criteria about it.

It is the responsibility of the public and the city to select, establish and maintain the standards of performance required of the public environment. Our planners cannot expect to exert adequate influence on the private environment controlled by individuals and corporations until it has set criteria for our shared environment, the public environment. Municipal authorities have the power to set performance criteria rather than to simply purchase products. Why not set such standards, for example, for the millions of dollars our cities will spend this year on streets and all their appurtenances, and then consider performance before rushing to the product catalogues. The limited amenity an individual can afford when they live in isolation is multiplied by thousands when they live in a community and a collective amenity is made possible. The entire system where these amenities can be cultivated consists of facilities for:

FREE AND CONVENIENT MOVEMENT OF ALL KINDS, ORIENTATION, LEARNING AND GUIDANCE
PROTECTION AND SHELTER AND LIGHTING AND COMFORT
RECREATION AND RELAXATION
THE INVITATION TO PURCHASE GOODS AND SERVICES
LEARNING

If the patterning and performances possible are made clear in the city – the city itself is then observable. Allowing the city to become observable gives its citizens the incredibly abundant gift of unlimited classrooms and the creation of an environment for learning. We can make mapping observable and work to understand their comparative patterns.

Standards set for the public environment would naturally and effortlessly affect the physical form of the entire private domain. The interface between the public environment and the private environment is both continuous and contiguous.

In fact, setting performance standards for proposals in the public environment and resolving to make the city observable can be made inseparable, and both must become mandatory tenets of our design vocabulary. I have again and again mentioned performance and not function. Function is the movement of our bowels – necessary, but not artful.

Performance standards for the total environment can be understood as a program for a theater of human endeavors. For this theater we need a stage and the determinants of this stage shape it. The stage is the public environment and the performances that artfully take place therein are continuous. The agglomeration of these performances is the daily life and image of the city.

An Urban Observatory or an Orchard of Understanding are revolutionary proposals really. One that would change appreciably the running of our governments and practically crumble the current modus operandi of our planning commission, police, budgets and infrastructure of our governments. It would do this by making public information public and comparative. My interest has since evolved into the more extensive concern of making the city itself observable. First, however, I shall describe the more measurable part of the proposal: the museum of the city; the Urban Observatory and the Orchard of Understanding.

Cities and countries can describe themselves to their citizens at all levels and for all comparative scales of comprehension. They can do this with enthusiasm, honesty, clarity and

ORCHARD OF UNDERSTANDING
Concept renderings of a multi-location, outdoor museum of understanding including work from the Urban Observatory, current events, and a ground floor arcade which allows for simultaneous transmission between locations. The various surfaces could be used for aquaria, views of space and late breaking news.

fun. Historically, people have chosen to set aside a place for objects and information pertaining to a particular phase or aspect of their civilization. These places have come to be known as museums. Museums can now be held in your hand. Without any doubt, the most significant part of our civilization—that which touches all aspects of our lives—is our urbanized environment. It is the city and its human-made environment with its sociological, economic and political realities that can clearly be described to the people living there. This might be done in a manner allowing all of humankind to sense the constraints of growth and change and the inter-relationships of elements. The content of which I speak embodies 3 major concerns:

FORMATION
SITUATION ASPIRATION
FORMATION IS THE HISTORICAL DEVELOPMENT OF THE REGION.

Formation includes the form and make-up of the region as well as the various relationships between political, social, economic, scientific and historical events. Two essential characteristics of formation are the recognition of the inevitable growth and change, and the concurrent idea of time. Where time is of over-riding importance, comprehension would be aided by the appropriate multiple visual modalities.

Situation is the present condition of the region. Situation is the annual, seasonal and daily life of the city. It describes what is presently happening within our schools, our people and our institutions. It includes the way we use our money as well as our use of land, air and water. Situation is also concerned with the location of housing, land use generally, urban renewal areas and all the movement systems which lace and connect the city.

One should be able to dial certain relationships: the inter-relationship between a highway program and residential development, or a school and the school-age population. The staff of the department of streets and board of education, as well as other city officials, might be invited to use this section making it an alive and working place. This would be the location of the urban gaming center.

Aspiration embodies future possibilities. Aspiration embodies the long and short range desires and plans of all institutions and departments of city government. This section of the museum becomes the public forum for the display and public testing of departmental ideas. It is a display that also can educate the public as to what might be, what should be, what could be.

The museum of the living city, or the Urban Observatory or the Orchard of Understanding, should be the visual data center of cities and countries. The city can be thought of as a real time, full sized museum of understanding.

Digital displays might allow each visitor to dial any relationship in the growth of these aforementioned elements through the history of the region and thereby see the various inter-relationships and correlations. Certainly the narration of such exhibits on growth should be steeped in the history of the region enabling school children to sense the context of the times. There should be current maps and models of all kinds describing quickly, clearly, and tangibly things like all houses for sale and their price ranges so that someone moving into or about the city might comprehensively and freely choose a place to live – and thus put into practice open housing. There should be similar displays to show industrial land and plant facilities; their magnitude and cost; the location of the unemployed; housing quality; total amount of personal income; its tax assessment; and age and population density. There should be descriptions of the availability and location of all public amenities, medical facilities and social help and so on.

The museum would act as a catalyst – the center for all public information as well as a working center for learning, inter-disciplinary and inter-departmental projects. This should be a place where proposed expressway routes and major roads could be shown so their effect on the social, economic and physical face of the city might be assessed in advance. It would be the visual forum for all physical improvements to the city and the initial site for all public announcements to the citizens of such plans.The observatory could extend a supplemental network throughout cities, with major nodes in the ground floor lobbies of all public buildings. The departments of the city would assume the previously ignored responsibility to describe particular aspects of the city to its citizens – creating an invitation to the comprehension of growth, scale, statistics, patterning and the aspirations of future plans for our urbanized world.

These various departments and institutions would thus embrace the responsible act of telling what and why they do what they do and think of the effect this action would have even if only the department of city planning, the departments of police and fire, and the department of streets participated! At the centroid of the city a museum could be a new urban institution connecting us in real time to a country's worldwide network. Its containing an invitation to all to be informed.

NIGHT RENDERINGS
Stills of the exhibit at night time.

RENDERINGS Hassan Husein

Prior to a turning point in my life, which was being asked to chair the Aspen Conference in 1970 and 1972 (the first kind of seminal movement from schlepper to player) was when I decided at 26, in my first teaching job as assistant professor of architecture at NC State Raleigh, NC to teach a little bit of geography to design students in a first-year architecture class. It came about because several of the students, when I mentioned Alvar Aalto and Helsinki, didn't know what Helsinki was, or really what Finland was, and were semi-proud of never having been above the Mason-Dixon line.

I thought it would be an interesting way to extend their vocabularies of cities and therefore architecture if they knew places of the world. I made a list of cities and sent them out to see if we could get maps, but they couldn't get many, either through the meager library or at that time, the primitive way you could find information. We got a list of cities, ancient and modern, and I just settled on a single scale. I made good decisions, but they were not scientific.

Cities: Comparisons of Form and Scale 1962

It turns out if I'd done it scientifically, I would've come up with the same things. I worked out a mass production way of dividing the cities into squares, so a small city could be one square and a big city could be up to 12 squares, and each could be worked on separately once they were laid out. A 17-by-17 inch piece of Masonite could be a square and we could work at one at a time on a table. I could get Plasticine and the tools we needed were just a group of nails wrapped in rubber bands for stippling trees, balsa wood we could push down to make roadways, black paint and ink for water. It was primitive. I knew I could photograph each one of them dead down, and at 17 inches you'd get no parallax. Then my friend, Gene Feldman, put those photographs through a half-tone screen made of enlarged paper fibers, so we had our own screen that was unique and made it look like sand. We could splice them together with just a little hairline joint between them to get a big plate. Each plate would be reduced by half so you'd get rid of all the maker's marks and inconsistencies, and would be spliced together into plates you could fold into an 8 1/2-inch square, which was the standard little student magazine they had.

I had no money; I think I borrowed a hundred bucks from my father. The school had no money. I was 26. They didn't know what the hell I was doing. I only had enough money for half the Plasticine, so when we were done with one half, we'd photograph it, scrape it off and use it for the second half. It was a tremendous learning curve for me of production, how to make something out of nothing, of comparative analysis, of the basic rule that what you can't just scientifically do, you just do. You just make those decisions, because with many decisions you'd spend the rest of your life deciding what they were and you wouldn't do any work. Well, we printed the book and it was magic. Within weeks, in what was viral for its time, we got feedback from around the world. Within months, it was on the cover of the top architectural magazine in Norway *L'Architecure d'Aujuord'hui* used one of the plates for its frontispiece, and the Yale School of Architecture mounted them and put them in an exhibit for about 25 years. I could not believe someone hadn't done this before. Such an obvious thing, and I thought, *Well, I'm just a pig in shit. I could do this the rest of my life.* I could just do things in a comparative manner and have a career and survive. That was very limited thinking on my part, but that's what I did for a little while. I did books that are mentioned in this one, *Various Dwellings Described in a Comparative Manner* and *The Urban Atlas: 20 American Cities*.

So, that thread I did when I was young has been the backbone of a lot of my work, and it happened from this little, thoughtful teaching device that came about in North Carolina. And which I'm still pleased about. In 2010, I spoke to 16,000 cartographers from 150 countries at the ESRI User Conference in San Diego. Using photography from Landsat, which ESRI owns and takes photos from space with, they put those photos over our original plates created from Plasticine 50 years ago by students at the University of North Carolina up on the screen, and let them fade one into the other – and they fit perfectly. It was a special moment in my life, it gave validity to something I had done when it seemed I was a child. **RSW**

AMSTERDAM

Capital of the Netherlands
North Holland Province on the river at
the mouth of the Amstel River;
fishing village dammed and
castellated in the early 13th century;
chartered in 1300 and world trade
center in the 17th century.

Elevation
8 feet

Population
1622: 105,000
1800: 201,000
1880: 317,000
1900: 511,000
1922: 606,484
1952: 845,266
1957: 871,188
1960: 866,300
1970: 820,406 (met. area: 1,035,999)
2011: 779,808

ANGKOR

Cambodia
North of Siemreap and near the north
shore of Lake Tonle Sap
Founded by Inravarman as the capital
of the Khymer Kingdon in the 9th
century; temple complex completed
in the 12th century; abandoned in
1443 after raids by the Chams and
the Thai; ruins discovered in 1860.
Reconstructed plan.

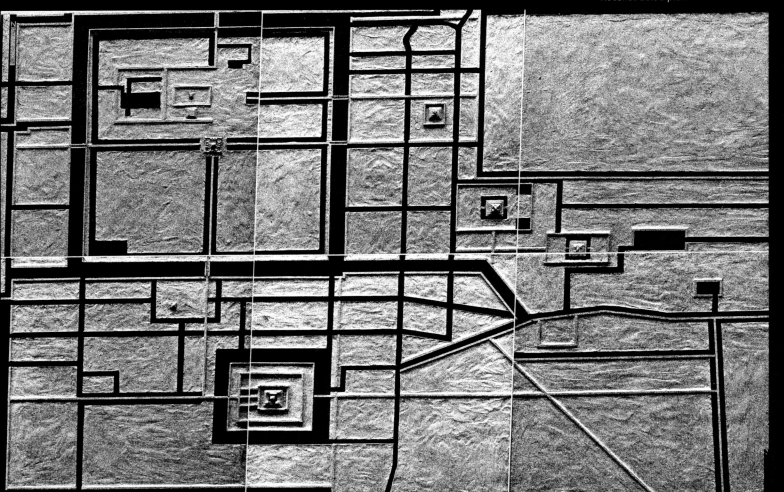

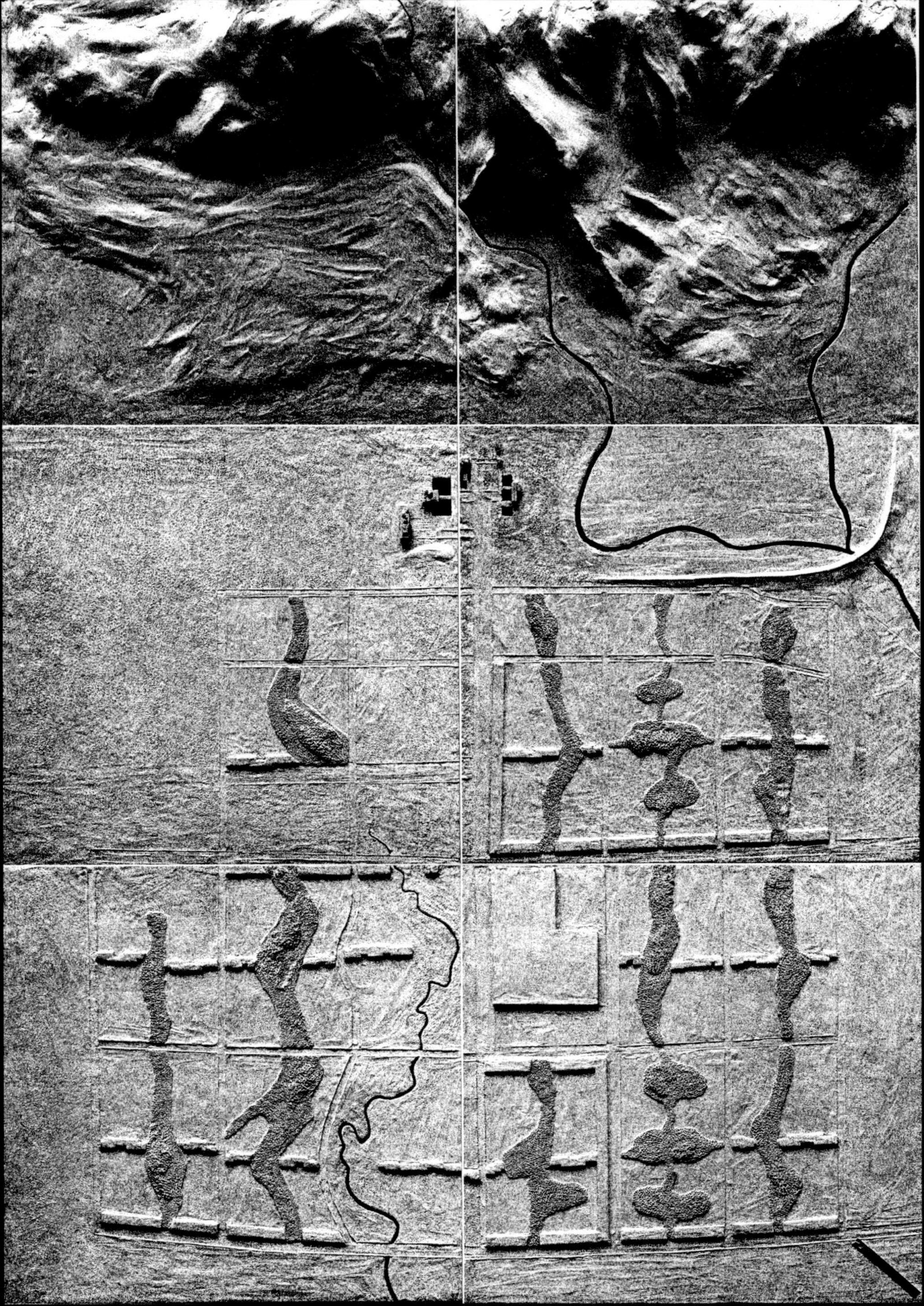

CHANDIGARH

India
Capital of Punjab, near the Ghaggar
River in the Ambala district.
Designer and consultant to the
project: Le Corbusier
Plan based on the 1951 scheme.

Population
1951: 5,294
1961: 89,321
1971: 256, 979
2001: 808,515
1st statge projection: 150,000
2nd stage projection: 500,000

13

Elevation
62 feet

Population
1909: 43,600
1929: 33,000
1952: 38,938
1958: 43,049
1971: 88,428
2006: 82,428

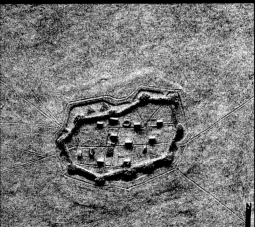

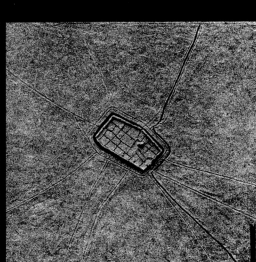

MONTAGNANA

Italy
Padua Province, Veneto
Fortified town with walls b
13th and 14th centuries.

Elevation
52 feet

Population
1930: 8,700
1950: 4,290
1958: 12,702
1968: 10,457
2011: 9,454

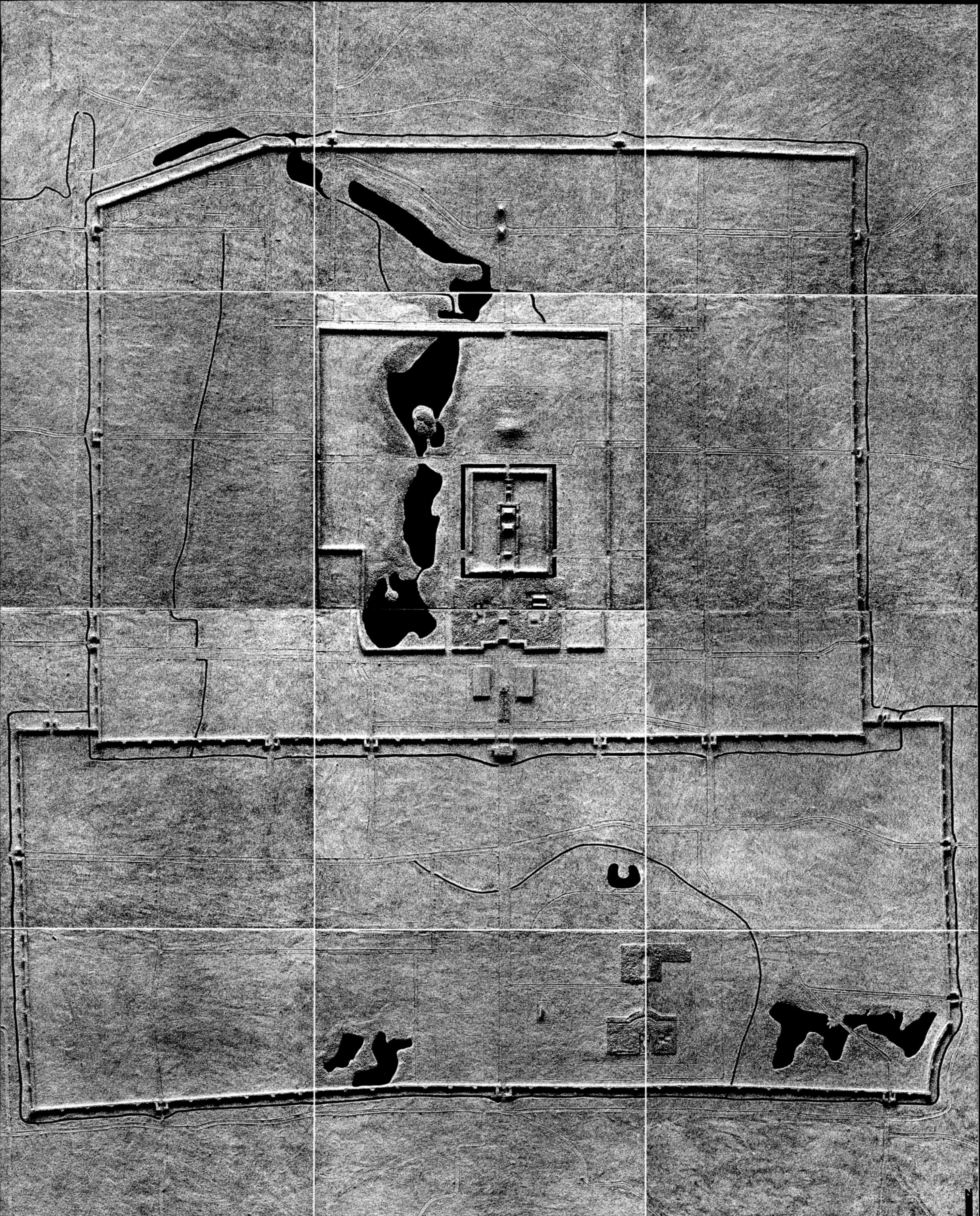

15

PEKING

Peiping, Pei-ching
Capital of China
North Hopeh Province
Capital of the Yen Kingdom of the
Chou Dynasty 222-110 B.C.; great
capital of the Liao Dynasty from 920
until it fell to the Golden Horde in
1122; enjoyed greatest grandeur
when Kublai Khan made it his capital
in 1267; called Cambalac by Marco
Polo; renamed Peking; it continued
as the capital of China from 1421 to
1928, and from 1949 to the present.

Elevation
165 feet

Population
1946: 1,672,438
1952: 1,940,290
1962: 4,060,000
     6,800,000*
1970: 4,010,000
     7,570,000*
2000: 11,510,000 (Beijing)
*inclluding extensive rural zones now
within Peking's municipal boundaires.

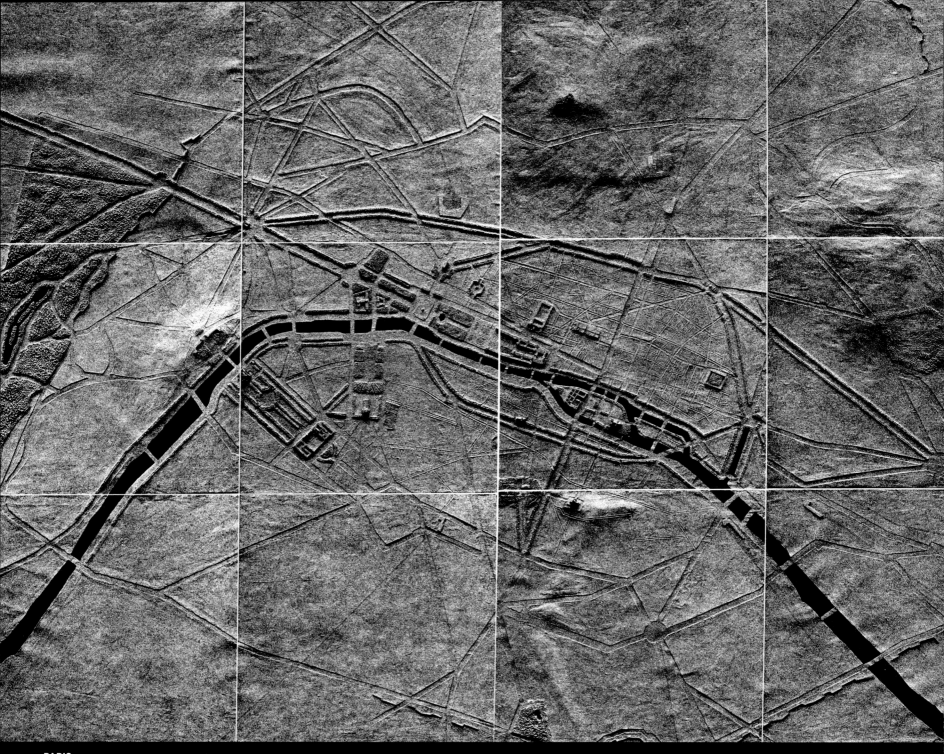

PARIS

Parisii
Capital of France
Capital of Seine Department, on the
Seine River, spanned by 33 bridges
After Caesar's conquest the Callic
fishing village on the Ile de la Cite
became Lutetia Parisiorum; became
a center of learning under Charlem-

and made capital of France by Hugh
Capet in 987; enjoyed greatest
prosperity in early 14th century;
Hausmann's plan implemented under
Napolean III.

Elevation
250 feet

Population
1250: 150,000
1675: 540,000
1715: 750,000
1800: 646,900
1861: 1,696,000
1906: 2,763,393
1921: 2,820,534

1972: 2,461,000
2010: 2,244,000

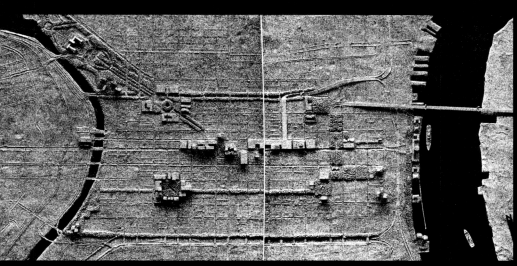

PHILADELPHIA

U.S.A
State of Pennsylvania
Founded 1682 as a Quaker colony
by William Penn: capital of the U.S.A.
from 1790-1800, as well as capital of
the Pennsylvania until 1799; first
occupied by the Lenni-Lenape Native
Americans. Projected comprehensive
plan by the City Planning
Commission, 1960.

Elevation
Sea level to 440 feet

Population
1890: 1,000,000
1940: 1,931,334
1950: 2,071,605
1960: 2,002,512
1970: 1,948,609
2013: 1,553,000

VENICE

Venezia
Capital of Venice Province, on the
Veneta Lagoon, 118 islands 2 1/2
miles from the mainland with 160
canals spanned by 400 bridges.
Founded in the 5th century by
refugees fleeing before Teutonic
invaders; organized under a doge
in 697; Basilica of San Marco begun
c. 14th and early 15th centuries; lost
its possessions in the 16th and 17th
centuries.

Elevation
6 feet

Population
1450: 200,000

1881: 132,000
1930: 183,700
1936: 170,830
1952: 204,484
1960: 336,184
1971: 360,241
2012: 260,060

VERSAILLES

France
Capital of Sein-et-Oise Department,
11 miles west-southwest of Paris
Site of hunting lodge built by Louis
XIII in 1629; selected as the site for
the new court palace for Louis XIV;
built between 1661 and 1682 by the
architects Le Vau, Mansart and Le
Brun with a park by Le Notre.

Elevation
460 feet

Population
1946: 63,114
1954: 72,038
1960: 91,619
1968: 90,829
2009: 86,447

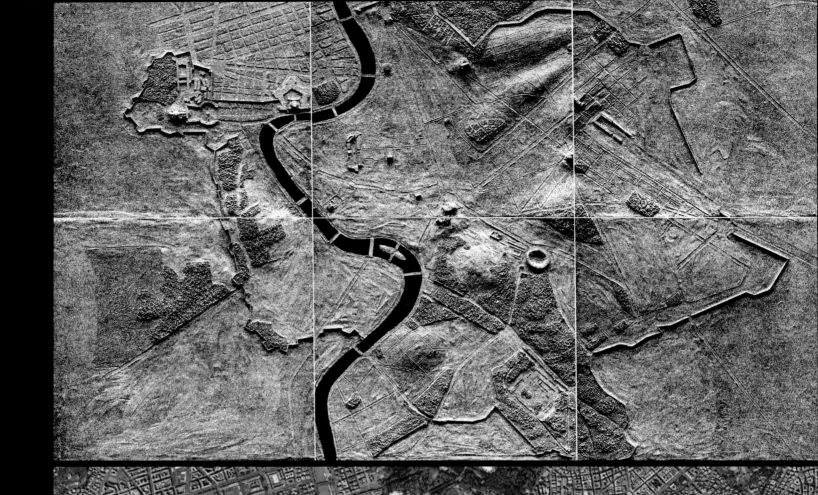

ROME

Roma
Capital of Italy
Capital of Rome Province, Latium
On both banks of the Tiber River, near Apenine Mountains
Traditionally founded by Romulus in 743 BCE; became capital of the Roman Republic and later of the Empire; capital of Italy since 1871 and site of Vatican City; master plan of Pope Sixtus V forms the basis of the development of Rome.

Elevation
44-462 feet

Population
1530: 30,000
1820: 148,000
1870: 245,000
1930: 960,000
1936: 1,089,996
1948: 1,613,660
1958: 1,935,041
1962: 2,175,000
1971: 7,799,836
2012: 2,627,000

LUBECK

Germany
Schleswig-Holstein
Founded by Count Adolph II of
Holstein in 1143; power of the
Hanseatic League in the 14th century

Elevation
Sea level

Population
1375: 85,000
1812: 22,722
1864: 34,500
1905: 51,005
1950: 238,276
1960: 232,100
1969: 242,855
2013: 211,713

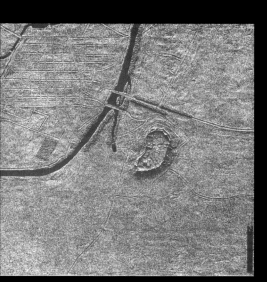

CARCASSONE

France
Capital of Aude Department, on the
Aude River and the Canal du Midi
Founded in the 5th century BCE by
the Iberians; medieval fortified town,
the stronghold of Al-bignenses;
pillaged and destroyed by the Black
Prince in 1355; restored by
Viollet-le-Duc in the 19th century.

Population
450: 1,000
1304: 9,500
1954: 31,305
1960: 37,305
1968: 43,616
2009: 47,854

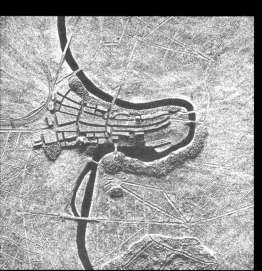

BERN

Berne
Capital of Switzerland
Capital of Bern Canton, on the Aar
River; Founded in 1191 CE by Duke
Berchtold V of Zahringen as a military
post; became the free imperial city of
Frederick II in 1218; was powerful in
the 18th century; made the capital of
Switzerland in 1848.

Elevation
1,876 feet (the old section is on a
ridge 115 to 130 feet high bounded
on three sides by the Aar River)

Population
1880: 45,000
1900: 67,000
1920: 105,000

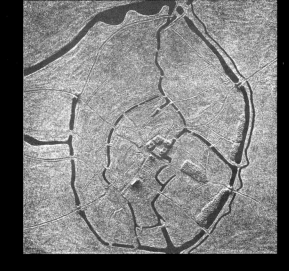

BRUGGE

Bruges (Flemish: "Bridge")
Belgium
Capital of West Flanders, at the mouth
of the Zwyn River on the North Sea
Founded in 865; a commercial and
artistic hub of Northern Europe in the
14th and 15th centuries; the sitting of
its access to the sea led to its decline
in the 16th century.

Elevation
Sea level

Population
1880: 50,000
1927: 53,000
1952: 51,805
1960: 52,278
1970: 51,303
2011: 117,377

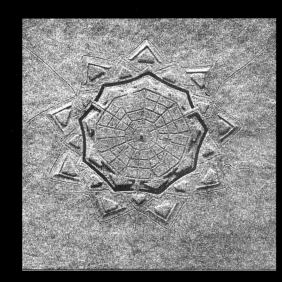

PALMANOVA

Palma Nuova
Italy
Udine Province, Friuli-Venezia Giulia
Founded in 1593, the Venetian
fortress was deigned by Scamozzi.

Elevation
98 feet

Population
1952: 3,237
1958: 5,845
1968: 6,437
2009: 5,406

TIKAL

My first hands on plane table mapping
experience. In 1958 or 1959, in the very first
season of reconstruction and clearing and
reconstitution of the largest and then-oldest of
the Mayan cities of the Peten jungle. There were
no roads into it, just some trees cut to make for
a rather dangerous landing strip. No electricity
of course, no running water, no doctor. Twelve of
us got into the jungle with a hand-cranked radio,
with which we were allowed to call the
president's office every day at 5 p.m., the only
contact we had with the real world. He was a
dictator we had put into power after we'd
fomented a revolution there. His name was
Ydigoras and he was like out of a cartoon. He
came in once with his machine-gun touting
bodyguards who started shooting at many of
the archeological ruins because they thought
it was great fun. I was there with 2 others to do
plane-table mapping of the city. I'd mapped
temples 3 and 4 and the juncture of the Mauslay
and Tozzer causeways, about a third of Tikal on
its southwestern quadrant. Surveyors there did
not use lasers; one used a slide rule and a log
of numbers. It was arduous and one of the most
uncomfortable experiences of my life.

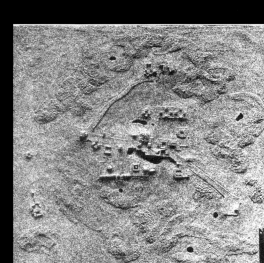

TIKAL

Guatemala
Department of Peten
Earliest settlement before 600 BCE;
earliest inscription dated 282 CE;
beleived to be the oldest and largest
of the Mayan cities, it was a great
religious and agricultural center;
abandoned after the disitegration of
classical authority ca. 900 CE
Plan from the Uiversity of
Pennsylvania Museum Survey

Elevation
600 feet

Population

800 CE: 10,000 in the central 16
square kilometers of the complex;
50,000 in the 130-square-kilometer
area surrounding the complex

WASHINGTON, D.C.

Capital of the U.S.A
District of Columbia
Site on the Potomac River chosen in
1791; designed by Pierre L'Enfant and
laid out by Andrew Ellicott
assisted by Thomas Jefferson; first
constructions were the White House
in 1792 and the Capitol in 1793;
sacked by the British in 1814; after
slow early growth, it assumed its
urban aspect only in the 20th century.

Elevation
Sea level to 420 feet

Population
1800: 14,093
1860: 75,080
1900: 278,718
1940: 663,091
1950: 802,178
1960: 763,956
1970: 756,510
2014: 658,893

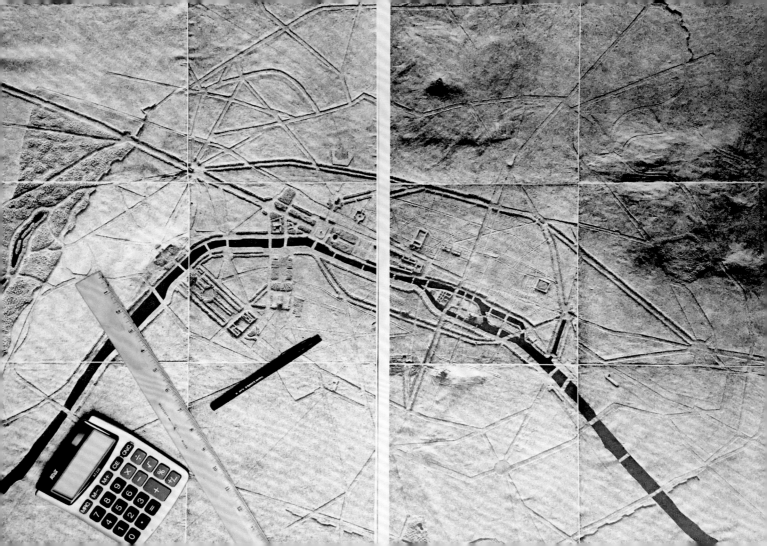

Angkor

Cambodia
North of Siemreap and near the north shore of
Lake Tonle Sap
Founded by Indravarman as the capital of
Khmer Kingdom in the 9th century; temple
complex completed in the 12th century; abandoned in 1443 after raids by the Chams and the
Thai; ruins discovered in 1860.
Reconstructed plan

Angkor: plan showing extent of seasonal flooding

...sin their municipal

8

–68,69,70,71,72,73

PARIS, Parisii
* Seine Dept. on Seine River, spanned by 33 bridges
* France
Founded 58-51 B.C. by Parisii Tribe
  After Caesar's conquest the Gallic fishing village on the Ile de la Cité
became a town Lutetia Partiorum, became center of learning under
Charlemagne, devastated 845-61, was refortified of France 987 by
Hugh Capet, greatest prosperity early 14th century. Hausman's plan
under Napoleon III
250
1250—150,000
1675—540,000
1715—750,000 est.
1800—546,856
1817—714,000
1851—1,053,000
1861—1,696,000
1906—2,763,393
1921—2,820,534
1954—2,906,000
1960—3,035,000

XXXI–B – 62,63,64,65,66,67

..., spanned by 33 br...

Sein...   ...sii Tribe
...B.C.   ...the Gallic fishing v...
...'s co... ...Parisiorum, becam...
...own 1... ...845-61, was ref...
...ne, de... ...osperity early 14...
...st, gre...
...poleon ...

...000
...000
...000 est.
...5,856
...4,000
...053,000
...696,000
...2,763,393
...2,820,534
...3,035,000

Cities: Comparisons of Form and Scale   Richard Saul Wurman

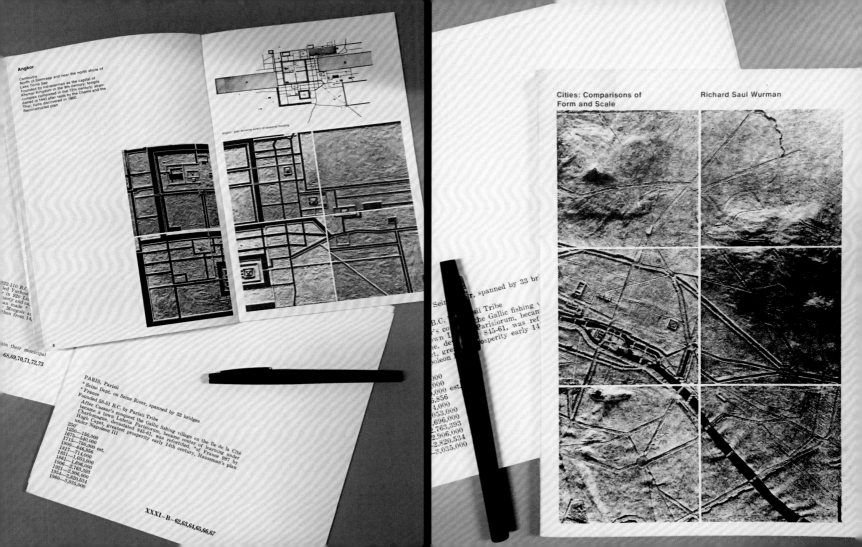

Urban Atlas
1967

I met Edwin Higbee through Governor Terry Sanford of North Carolina, who later became president of Duke University, when I was 26. Ed was an urban geographer who came to my class, heard me talk and saw a book I'd done on comparison of cities. When he got his next round of money from the 20th Century Fund, he wrote me into the grant to travel with him in 2- to 3-week trips to the major cities in the United States, meeting the mayors and heads of city planning, sometimes police commissioners and others – the potentates of various cities who had something to do with planning.

We even spent half a day with Harry S. Truman in his library in Independence, Missouri. I was looking at him like he was in Madame Tussaud's museum; I'd seen so many photographs of him that looking at him didn't seem real, I just looked at him with this glazed gaze. In any case, I had all this stuff sent back to me and it became the basis for my later analysis and development of *The Urban Atlas: 20 American Cities*. I'd brought the material to Dean Joseph Passonneau of the School of Architecture at the University of Washington, St. Louis, which turned into this atlas that was published by MIT Press.

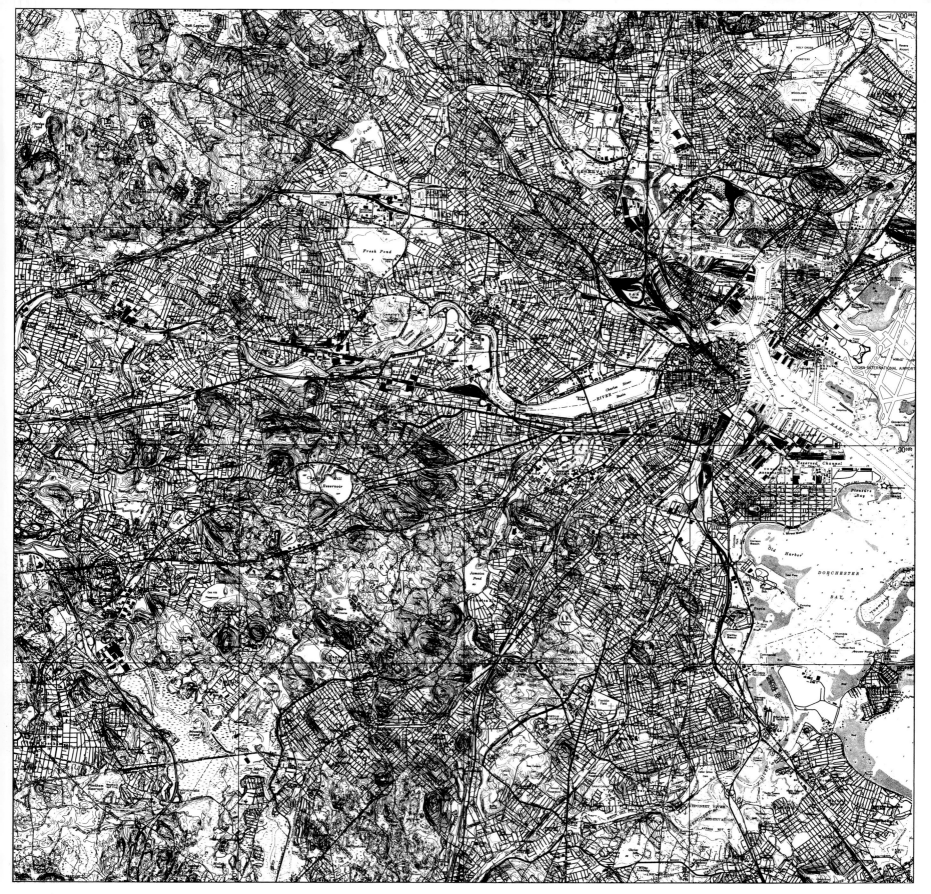

BOSTON Pieced together USGS transparencies of the center city, 1967.

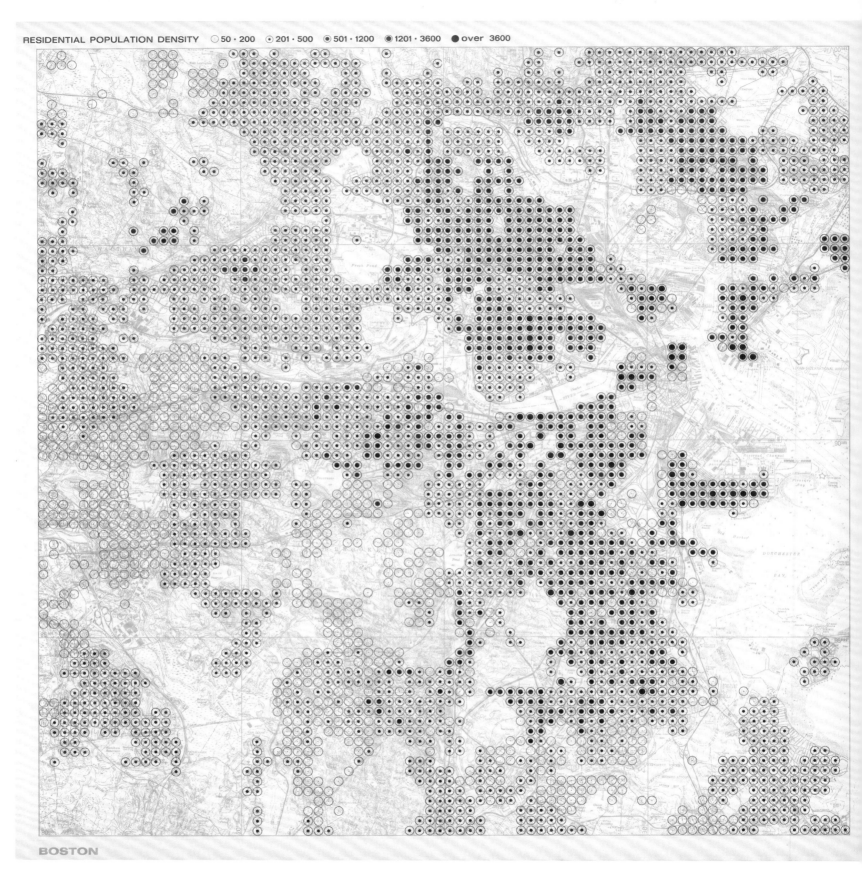

RESIDENTIAL POPULATION DENSITY ○ 50 · 200 ⊙ 201 · 500 ◉ 501 · 1200 ◉ 1201 · 3600 ● over 3600

BOSTON Residential Population Density

RESIDENTIAL POPULATION DENSITY   ○ 50 · 200   ⊙ 201 · 500   ⊙ 501 · 1200   ⊙ 1201 · 3600   ● over 3600

AIRPORT-CEMETARY   INSTITUTIONAL   PARK   LARGE INSTITUTIONAL

27

□ INDUSTRIAL   ▢ COMMERCIAL

BOSTON Residential Population Density | Industial v. Commercial

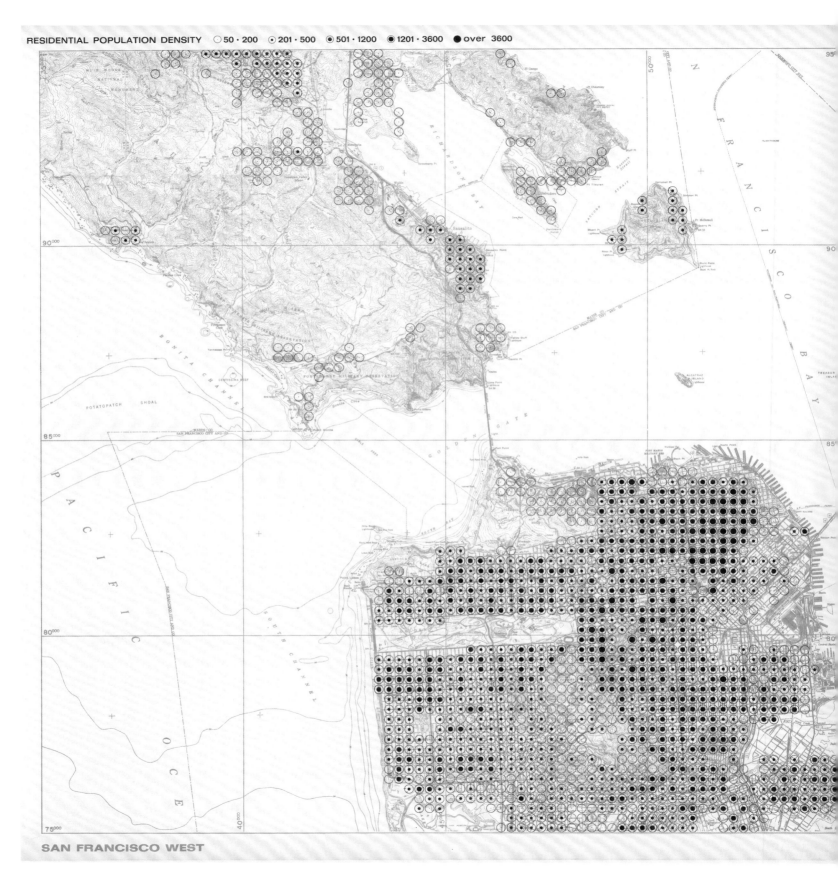

RESIDENTIAL POPULATION DENSITY ○ 50 · 200 ⊙ 201 · 500 ◉ 501 · 1200 ◉ 1201 · 3600 ● over 3600

SAN FRANCISCO WEST Residential Population Density

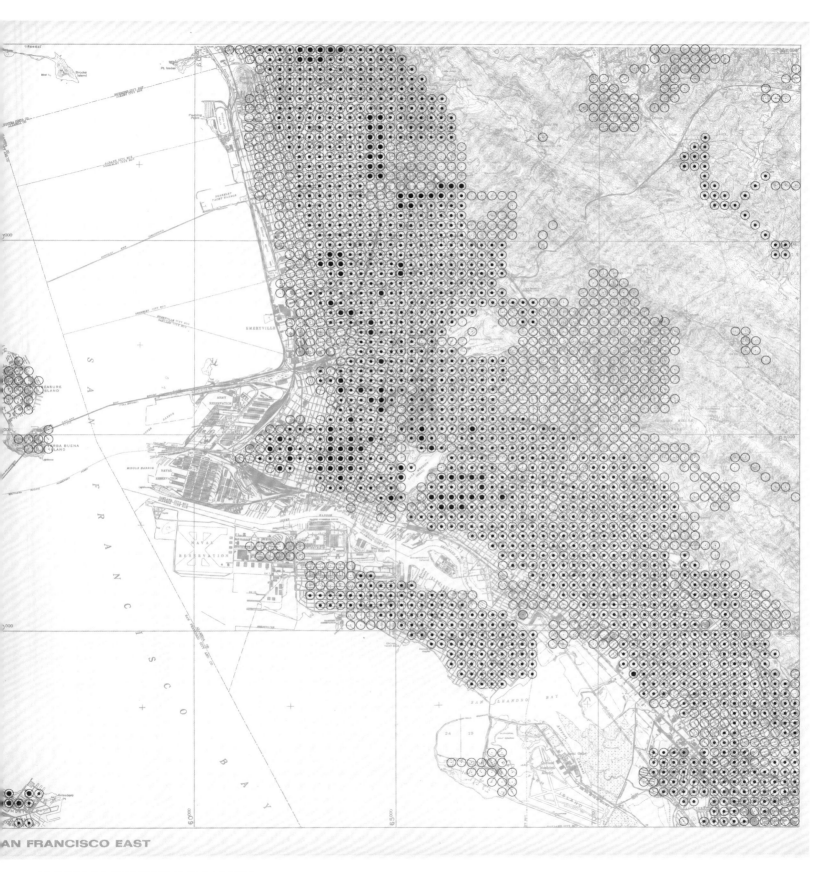

AN FRANCISCO EAST

SAN FRANCISCO EAST Residential Population Density

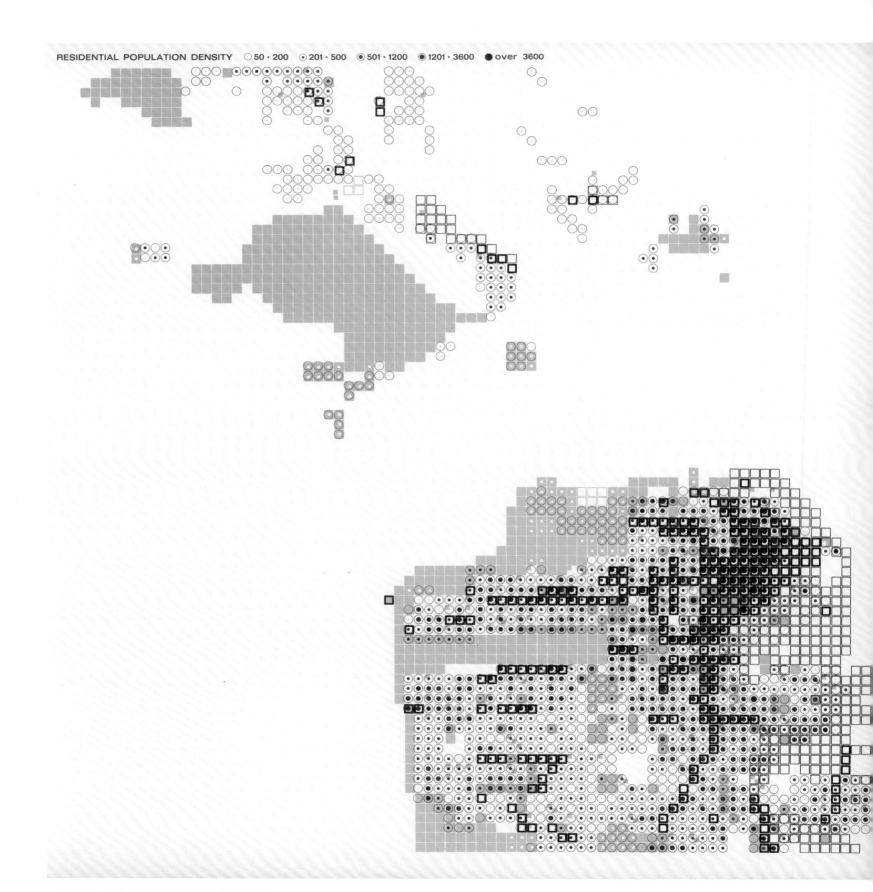

SAN FRANCISCO WEST Residential Population Density | Industial v. Commercial

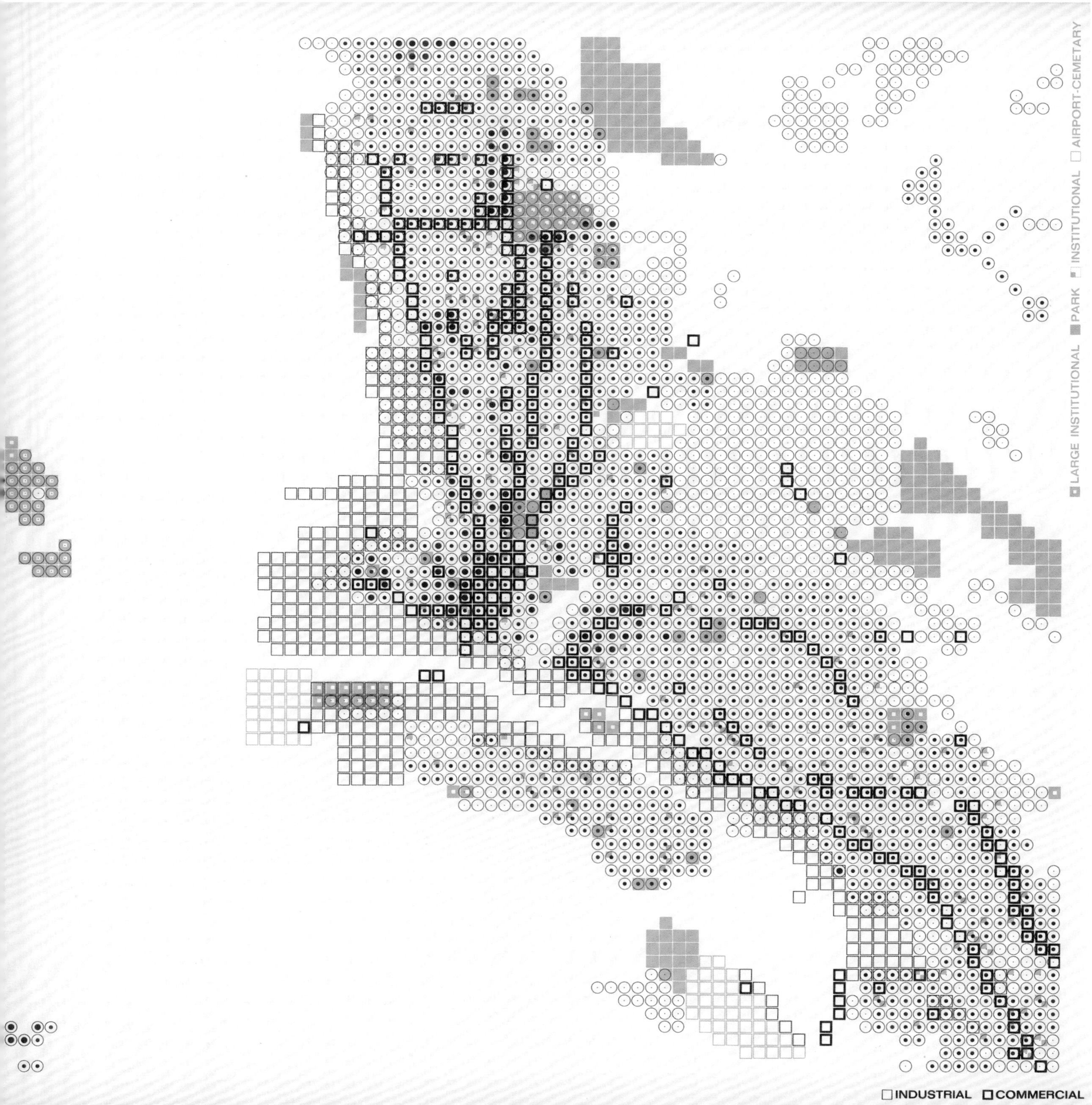

LARGE INSTITUTIONAL PARK INSTITUTIONAL AIRPORT-CEMETARY

INDUSTRIAL COMMERCIAL

SAN FRANCISCO EAST Residential Population Density | Industial v. Commercial

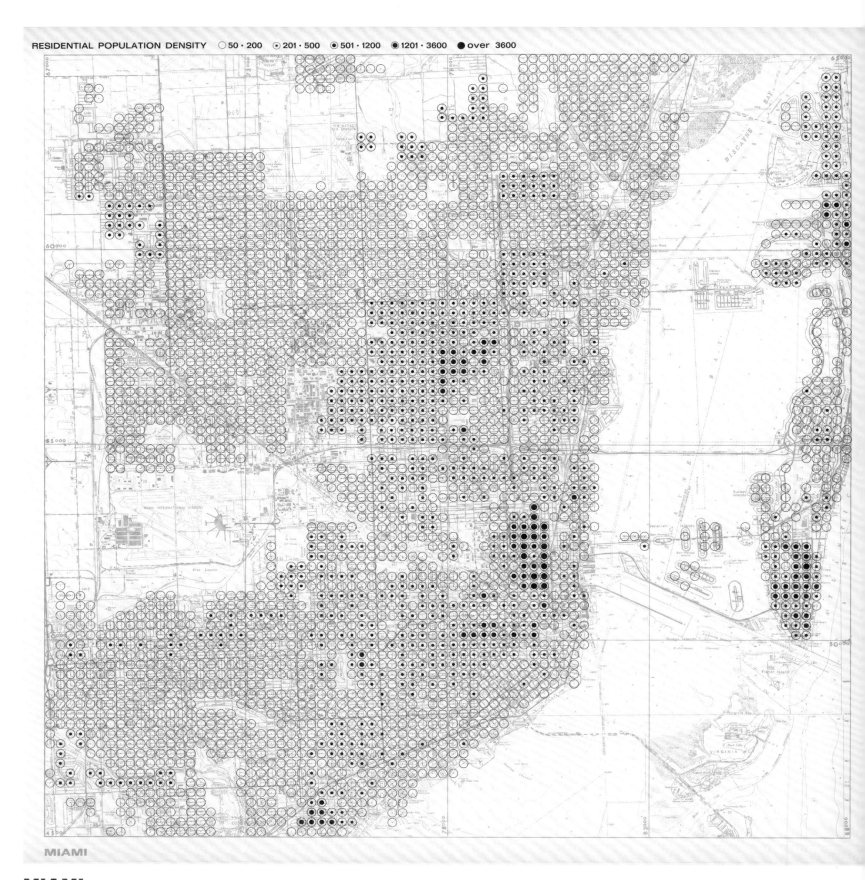

RESIDENTIAL POPULATION DENSITY ○ 50 · 200 ◎ 201 · 500 ◉ 501 · 1200 ◉ 1201 · 3600 ● over 3600

MIAMI

MIAMI Residential Population Density

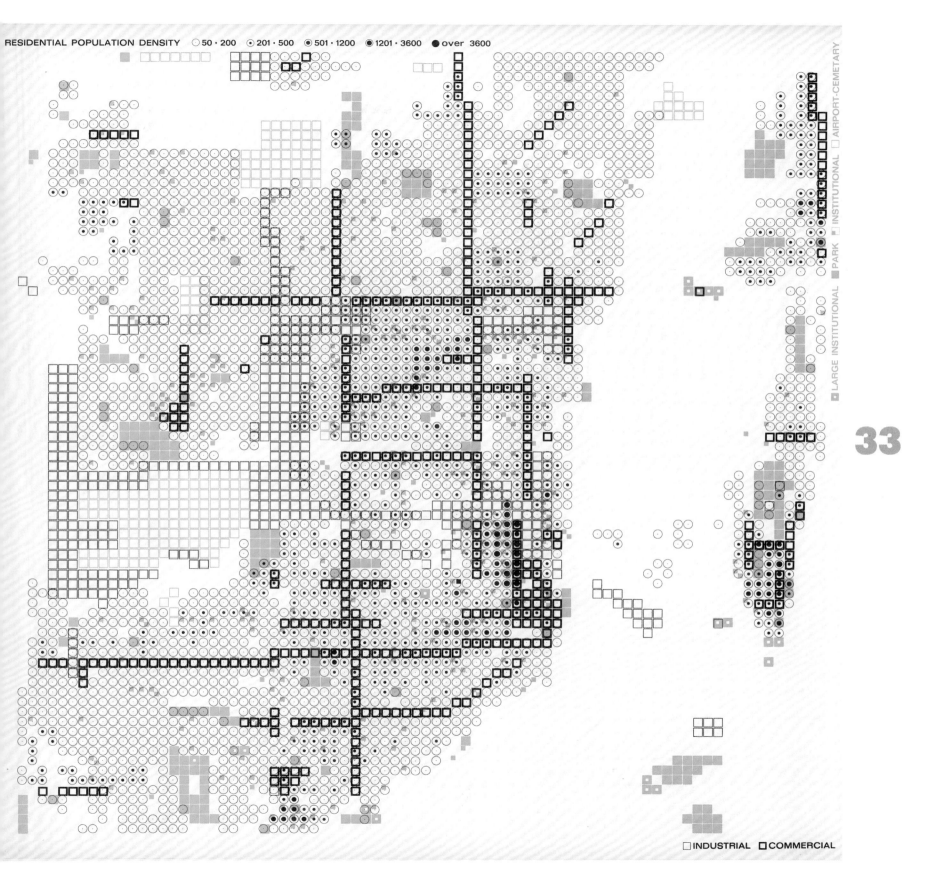

RESIDENTIAL POPULATION DENSITY ○ 50·200 ⊙ 201·500 ◉ 501·1200 ◉ 1201·3600 ● over 3600

AIRPORT-CEMETARY

INSTITUTIONAL

PARK

LARGE INSTITUTIONAL

33

□ INDUSTRIAL □ COMMERCIAL

MIAMI Residential Population Density | Industial v. Commercial

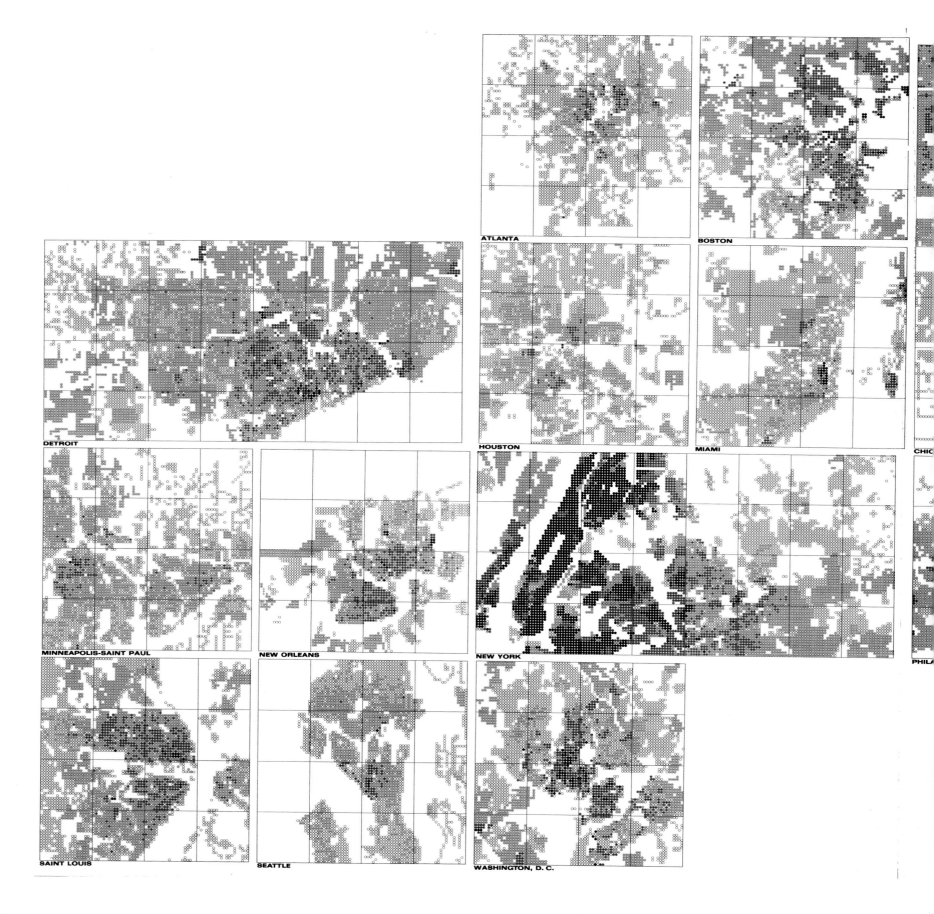

ATLANTA

BOSTON

DETROIT

HOUSTON

MIAMI

CHIC

MINNEAPOLIS-SAINT PAUL

NEW ORLEANS

NEW YORK

PHILA

SAINT LOUIS

SEATTLE

WASHINGTON, D. C.

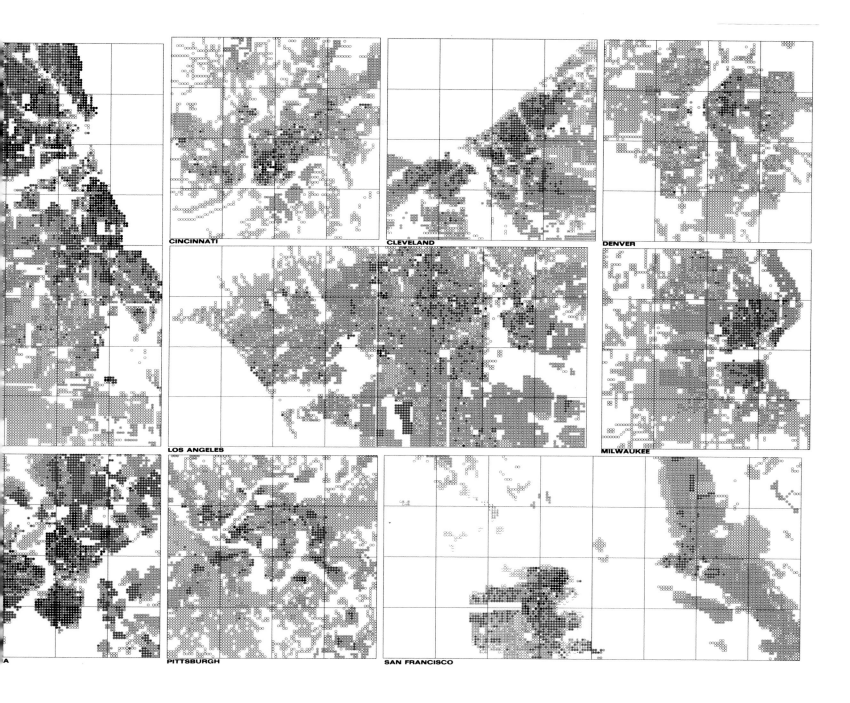

CINCINNATI

CLEVELAND

DENVER

LOS ANGELES

MILWAUKEE

PITTSBURGH

SAN FRANCISCO

35

These maps describe residential land use and population density.

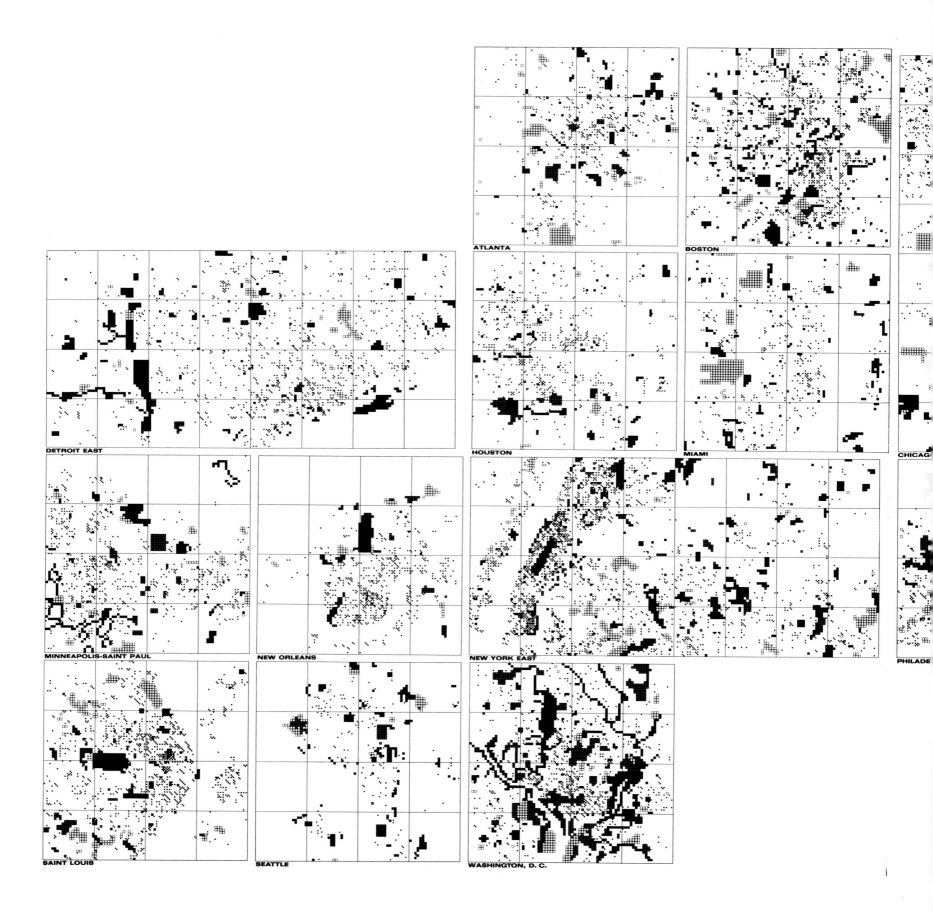

ATLANTA

BOSTON

CHICAG[O]

DETROIT EAST

HOUSTON

MIAMI

MINNEAPOLIS-SAINT PAUL

NEW ORLEANS

NEW YORK EAST

PHILADE[LPHIA]

SAINT LOUIS

SEATTLE

WASHINGTON, D. C.

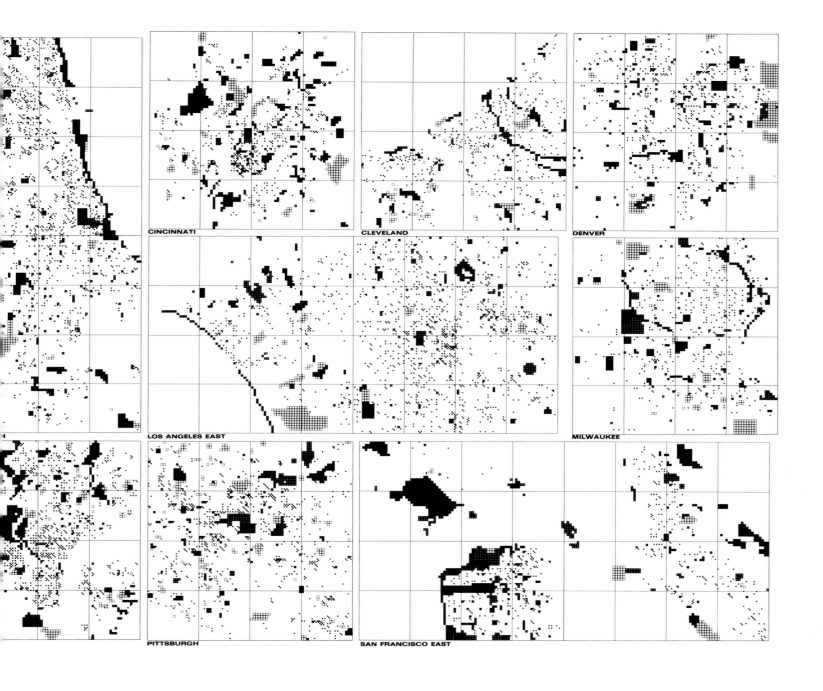

CINCINNATI CLEVELAND DENVER

LOS ANGELES EAST MILWAUKEE

PITTSBURGH SAN FRANCISCO EAST

These maps describe park and industrial land use.

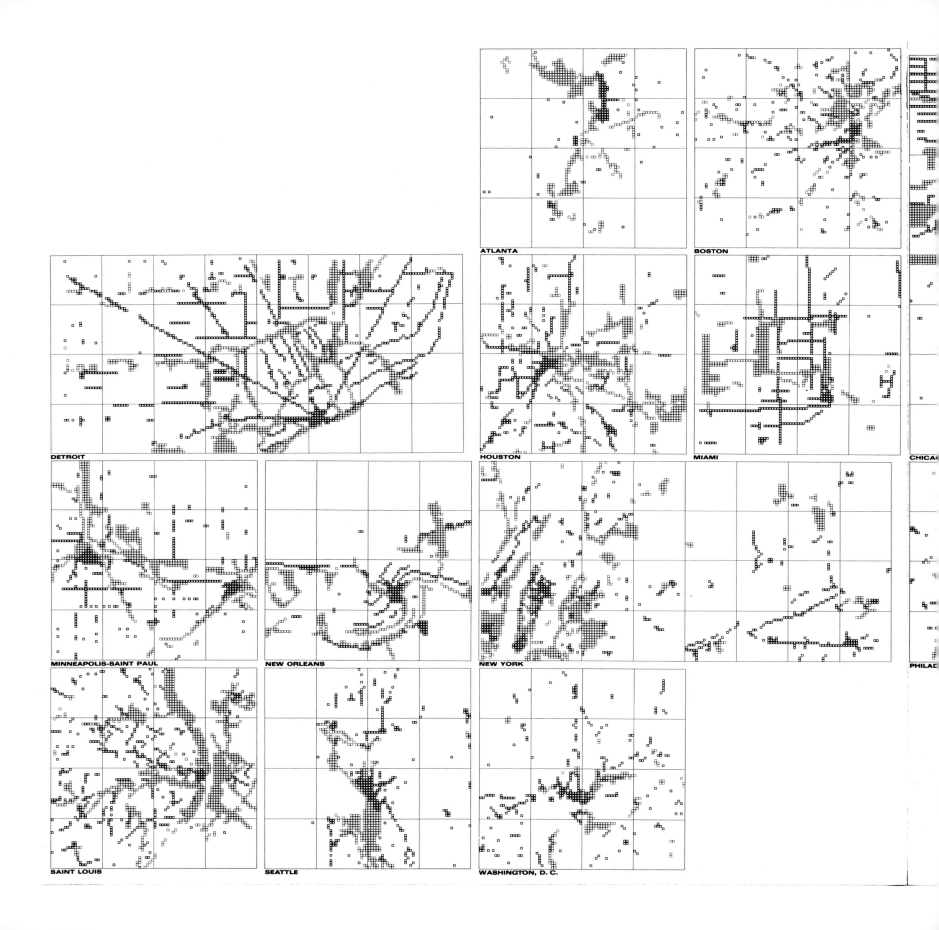

ATLANTA

BOSTON

PHILAD

DETROIT

HOUSTON

MIAMI

CHICA

MINNEAPOLIS-SAINT PAUL

NEW ORLEANS

NEW YORK

PHILAD

SAINT LOUIS

SEATTLE

WASHINGTON, D. C.

CINCINNATI

CLEVELAND

DENVER

LOS ANGELES

MILWAUKEE

PITTSBURGH

SAN FRANCISCO

39

These maps describe commercial and industrial land use.

Man-Made
Philadelphia
1972

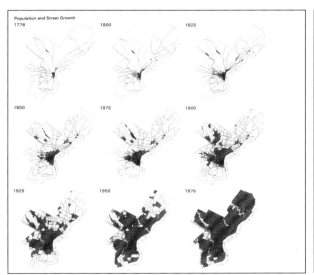

1850   1875   1900

1925   1950   1976

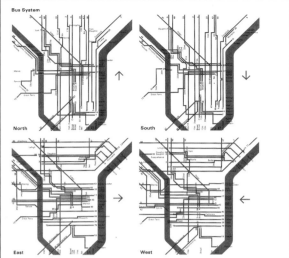

Bus System

North   South

East   West

26

Benjamin Franklin Parkway

The construction of the Benjamin Franklin Parkway in the early twentieth century was the only significant modification of the grid plan of William Penn. The parkway was originally proposed in 1892 and consisted, even in the initial plans, of a baroque boulevard intended to create a diagonal vista that would break the monotony of the grid plan. After many delays the parkway concept was taken up in 1910 by the Fairmount Park Art Association, which engaged French landscape designer Jacques Greber to create the final plan. Greber's plan produced the desired uninterrupted vista from Faire Mount (as the slight hill at the western end was historically known), where a new art museum was to be erected, to the City Hall Tower.

Following Greber's plan, a new design for the Art Museum was approved and construction begun on the east and west wings while fund-raising went on for the center portion. Some parts of the building have still not been completed. Construction of the Parkway itself began in 1917 and proceeded from west to east. The western end was modeled after the Champs Elysees with wide roads, many rows of trees, and substantial setbacks for the buildings. Few of the suggested buildings were ever completed, with two notable exceptions, the Philadelphia Museum of Art and the modest Rodin Museum and Courtyard, a substitute for a more grandiose proposal. The plaza and fountains in front of the Art Museum were begun, but redesigned and completed in 1967. The present appearance of this part of the Parkway is dominated by several recent apartment buildings.

The central section of the Parkway required the complete redesign of Logan Circle and is described in Section 2. The eastern section is intentionally more urban, and the narrow spatial connection to City Hall, proposed by Greber, has been accomplished in recent years by the addition of several new apartment buildings, the United Fund Office Building, the Friends Select School, and the Pennwalt Office Building. Originally, the Parkway terminated at City Hall. This arrangement changed in the 1950s coincident with the development of Penn Center. The last block was closed to traffic, and John F. Kennedy Plaza on top of an underground parking garage became the new terminus. A national competition was held for the design of a fountain for this plaza, but the winning proposal was never built, and the present pool and spray were substituted in its place.

Benjamin Franklin Parkway
12 Academy of Natural Sciences
13 ASTM Building
5 Bell Telephone Bldg.
15 Cathedral of SS Peter and Paul
1 City Hall
2 City Municipal Services Bldg.
25 Eastern State Prison
28 Fidelity Mutual Life Insurance Bldg.
18 Franklin Institute
23 Franklin Motor Inn
17 Free Library of Phila.
8 Friends Select School
6 Insurance Co. of N. America
4 Kennedy Plaza
14 Moore College of Art
29 Old City Waterworks
22 Parktowne Place Apts.
24 Parkway House Apts.
3 Penn Center
7 Pennwalt Corporation Bldg.
19 Phila. Board of Education
16 Phila. County Courthouse
26 Phila. Museum of Art
11 Plaza Apts.
21 Rodin Museum
27 The Philadelphian Apts.
9 United Fund Bldg.
10 Windsor Apts.
20 Youth Study Center
30 2601 Parkway Apts.

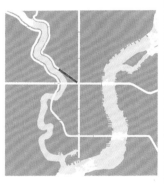

The first time I got serious about guidebooks was with Man-Made Philadelphia. John Andrew Gallery was head of housing and community development in Philadelphia, and later became my boss when I became assistant director in the department, and I decided to do a guide to Philadelphia. I blocked it out, designed it and he did the research and writing. I got a friend of mine, George Krause, to take the photos. This is when I was enamored with fish-eye cameras, and started to do my versions of Paris and some other maps, which were these kind of aerial perspectives to pull out. The construct of the book is interesting, and I got my feet wet.

The construct wasn't as sophisticated nor as brief as my later Access books, it was much more cocktail-tabley in a minor way, but it broke the city down into neighborhoods, looked at the transportation system; I developed the transportation system maps for the city and the diagrammatic maps based on the Beck subway maps of London. So some of the principles that I took further on in various books were certainly developed in this one book, of taking you through understanding micro and macro and movement and area. **RSW**

41

Plans for Philadelphia
Penn's Plan 1682

William Penn looked upon his grant of lands in America as an opportunity to conduct a "Holy Experiment." He proposed to found a society based upon justice and tolerance and chose to name the city Philadelphia for its Greek meaning, "City of Brotherly Love."

The original city was located at the narrowest part of the peninsula, between the Delaware and Schuylkill rivers. The plan was laid out for Penn by his surveyor, Thomas Holme, in 1682. The area covered was 1,280 acres, and the boundaries to the north and south were the present Vine and South streets. Holme's plan differed substantially in execution from Penn's initial idea of a green country town with houses set in the middle of large plots of land. Under the influence of military camps and English towns, particularly Londonderry, Holme laid out a rigid grid system of streets. He gave purchasers narrow lots in the city and compensated for this with free lots in the Liberty Lands to the north of the city.

Two main thoroughfares approximately bisected the town, High Street (now Market Street) and Broad Street. At their intersection a center square of ten acres was set aside for the town hall. In the center of each of the four quadrants, eight-acre squares were set aside for the common use and enjoyment of all the citizens.

Penn was a real estate entrepreneur. He offered initial purchase lots along both riverfronts and tried to encourage development to move inward thereby increasing the value of the land he continued to own.

After the revolution all of Penn's land was taken over by the Commonwealth and sold off rather rapidly. The Liberty Lands of North Philadelphia were quickly developed on a speculative basis, with rows of identical builders' houses. In Center City the back alleys designed for service access were declared public streets, which encouraged further subdivision of the small city lots and laid the foundation for present street plan and traffic problems. Small three-story houses with one room per floor (popularly known as "Father-Son-Holy Ghost" houses) were built on the backs of lots in these small alleys, further adding to the problems of congestion.

Cities planned in advance of the construction of the first buildings are comparatively rare. In colonial America, none was as carefully planned as Philadelphia. Beyond the central city Penn was concerned about the connections to other areas and made sure that roads were laid out before the land was divided among the various purchasers.

Penn's Plan 1682

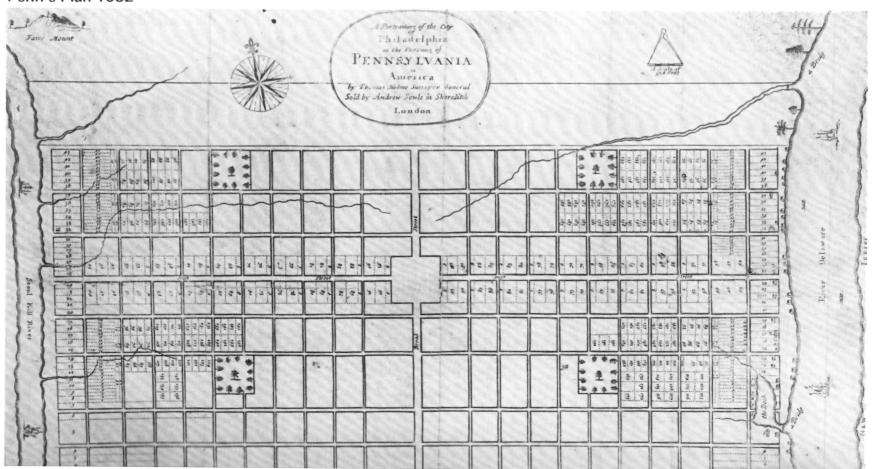

Most of these roads remain in the present plan of the city. In addition to the Liberty Lands Penn established eight manors outside the city, given mainly to his family, to control expansion. To persons with a similar background, he also sold townships, generally around 5,000 acres, which could in turn be sold by lots to individuals. The most successful of these was Germantown; Radnor, Merion, and Haverford townships were also started in this way.

Philadelphia grew steadily within the context of Penn's plan of 1682. The fact that Penn's heirs continued to hold large pieces of real estate until 1790 almost ensured that his vision would be realized. In succeeding decades few changes were made, as can be seen in the plan prepared by John Hill, surveyor and draftsman, in 1796. It was not until 1960 that a major new plan for Philadelphia was developed under the auspices of the revitalized City Planning Commission.

1796 Plan

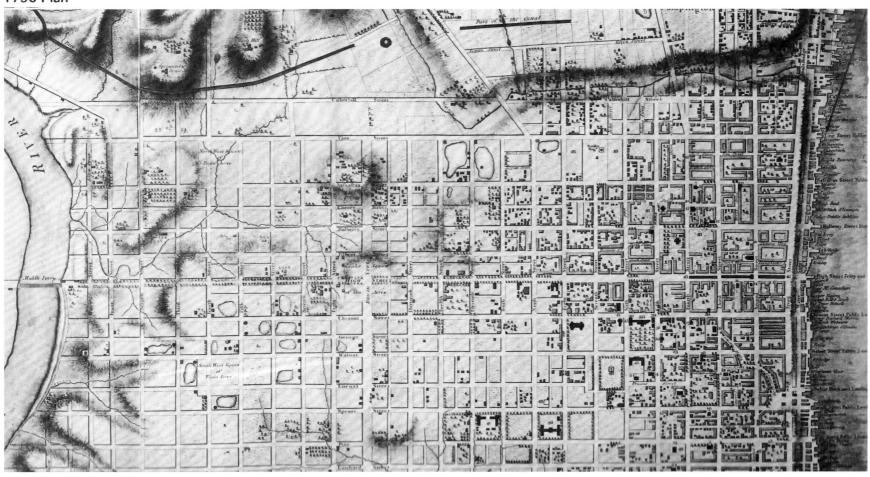

Citizens' Plans 1960–1970

The extensive urban renewal program begun in the 1950s drew many architects to the city and involved them in major projects. Many, however, were as concerned with the total character of the urban environment as the City Planning Commission and expressed that commitment in plans that went beyond concern for single buildings in conception. The Planning Commission had asked Louis I. Kahn to develop ideas for the Market Street East area, and from this beginning Kahn gradually expanded his work to consider all of Center City. Under a grant from the Graham Foundation, he developed a series of ideas including a hierarchical pattern of street movements, coupled with a system of parking garages (harbors).

While few of the ideas in Kahn's plan found their way into public policies, his personal Philadelphia plan provided a precedent for many young designers in the late 1960s when the city began considering ideas for a major celebration in 1976. At least eight citizen groups produced plans for the location of bicentennial activities or for an international exposition. The Committee for an International Exposition in Philadelphia in 1976 produced a plan for the Thirtieth Street area, which was subsequently adopted as public policy but was then succeeded by a series of other plans developed by the Philadelphia 1976 Bicentennial Corporation.

**Center City Plan
Louis Kahn**

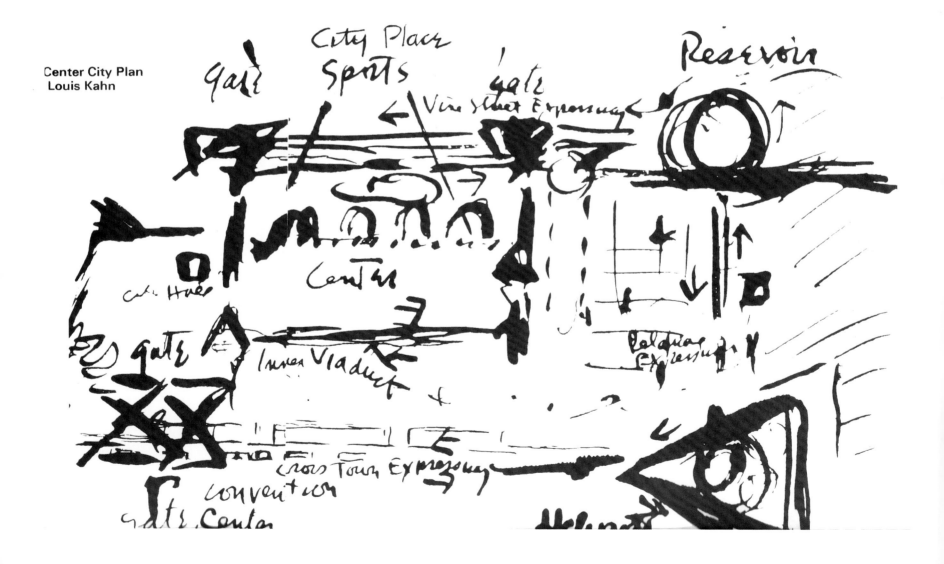

Center City Plan 1972

The Center City Plans of 1960-1963 indicated
preliminary ideas for the major downtown
projects. By 1972 these plans had changed
considerably; nevertheless, many original projects
are now complete. Others have undergone substantial redesign and are now nearing construction, but almost all of the projects identified
in 1960-1963 can be seen in one stage or another
throughout Center City. Many that were not
identified in the early plan have developed
as a result of publicly initiated projects. These
include the Hahnemann and Jefferson Medical Centers, Washington Square West residential community renewal, and the Franklin
Town Project. Only one major project of the
1960-1963 plan—the Market East Transportation
Center—remains in the planning stage.

1972 Plan

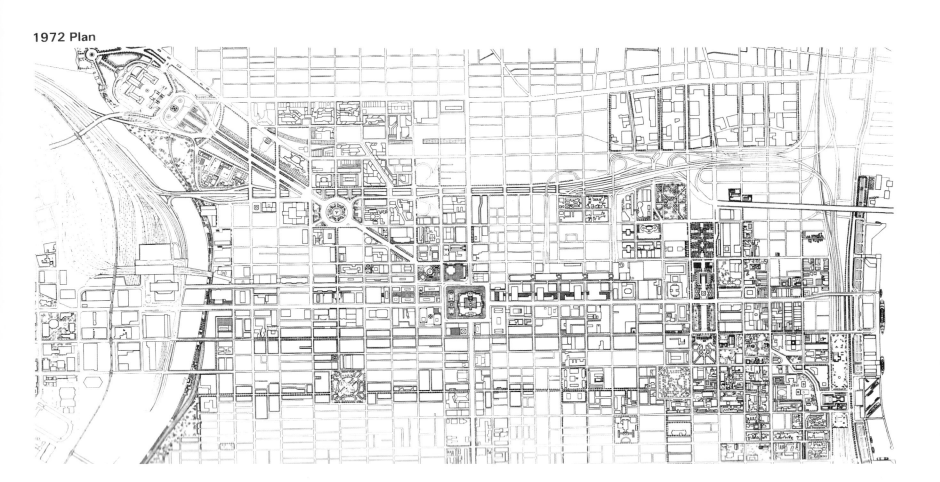

Cover Painting Robert Kulicke

Access Guides
1980s-2000s

I moved to Los Angeles in 1979 and it was frightening. I didn't know people, the road systems or the city. It's frightening for me to not understand where I am. I imagine it's frightening for everybody but they just don't talk about it because it makes them seem like a wuss. But it was frightening for me and I couldn't find a good guidebook. And this series of things came together, a vortex around my ignorance and my lack of understanding and orientation as well as it being around the 200th anniversary of the city's founding.

Cover Photography (Tokyo, Rome, Paris) Reven Wurman

The major figures of Renaissance Italy never heard of the tomato. In fact, the first three-quarters of Roman history were tomato-less: the "love apple" (so-called because of its supposed amorous properties) made its first appearance when it was brought from the New World at the turn of the 16th century.

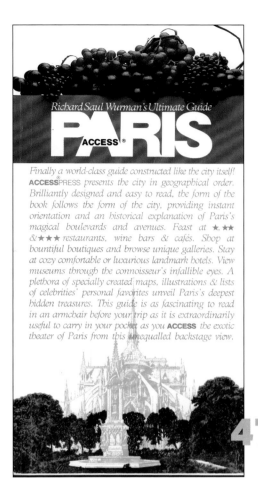

Richard Saul Wurman's Ultimate Guide

Finally a world-class guide constructed like the city itself! **ACCESS**PRESS presents the city in geographical order. Brilliantly designed and easy to read, the form of the book follows the form of the city, providing instant orientation and an historical explanation of Paris's magical boulevards and avenues. Feast at ★, ★★ & ★★★ restaurants, wine bars & cafés. Shop at bountiful boutiques and browse unique galleries. Stay at cozy comfortable or luxurious landmark hotels. View museums through the connoisseur's infallible eyes. A plethora of specially created maps, illustrations & lists of celebrities' personal favorites unveil Paris's deepest hidden treasures. This guide is as fascinating to read in an armchair before your trip as it is extraordinarily useful to carry in your pocket as you **ACCESS** the exotic theater of Paris from this unequalled backstage view.

47

At the time, a contact with Atlantic Richfield oddly arose, one of the biggest companies in the city. They gave me some money to do a guidebook; I sold it to them knowing I was ignorant of the city - a strange con at the time

The fundamental lesson in life as taught in schools is you sell your expertise. When you sell your expertise, you have a limited repertoire. If you sell your ignorance, you have an unlimited repertoire. My repertoire is unlimited because I sell my ignorance. My ignorance is what I sold and they paid for it. My ignorance was in not understanding the city. They paid for my personal journey from not understanding to understanding and that's the guidebook. The guidebook is how I wanted to understand. It wasn't trying to improve on any other guidebook.

It was starting from zero and saying, *How would I like to understand this city? What would my journey be? What were my needs and desires to find patterns of stuff that I would want to use and how to get there? And when I was someplace, what was around me?*

That's Access Guides, the opposite of how everybody sells a product because I sold ignorance, not intelligence, a book that was nonfiction, a journey of understanding, and that journey between 2 covers is the product. Access Press Guides became wanting to know where I was and what was around me.

RSW

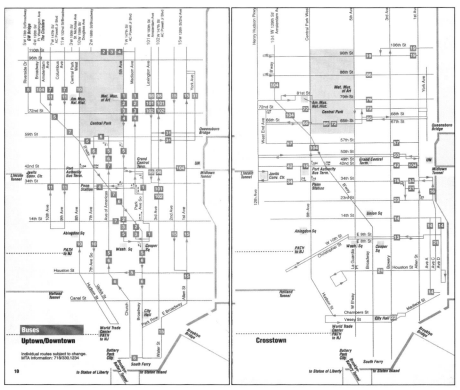

Lower Manhattan

It all began in **Lower Manhattan**, bounded by **Chambers St** and the **East** and **Hudson** rivers. Here, at the confluence of these majestic rivers, the earliest explorers —Giovanni Verrazano, Esteban Gómez and Henry Hudson—first touched land.

And it was here, in 1664, that the Dutch set up **Fort Amsterdam** to protect the southern perimeter of their settlement, called *Nieuw Amsterdam*. The skyscrapers and canyons of today's **Financial District** stand where once the tiny Dutch settlement, and later the prime residential enclave of post-Revolutionary New York, flourished.

The narrow alleys of the Financial District are a reminder of the scale of colonial America. But, except for a few fragments of old foundations, not a single building erected during the 40 years of Dutch rule remains. When the British Army withdrew in 1783 after 7 years of occupation, the village of New York—which covered 10 blocks north from the Battery—lay almost totally in ruins. But once New York City pulled itself together and began to push north, it grew in swift strides. Two blocks of low-rise commercial buildings from this early surge of development have survived: the **Fraunces Tavern** block and **Schermerhorn Row**.

When **City Hall**, the one still in use today, was being built in 1811 on the northernmost fringe of town, it seemed economically prudent to face the north side with common brownstone instead of marble, because no one ever expected the building to be seen from that side. But by 1820, New York City had expanded another 10 to 15 blocks, and by 1850, the limits had pushed 2 miles north to 14th St. A fire in 1835 leveled most of Lower Manhattan, but even that didn't halt the expansion of what had become the leading commercial center and port in the new country after the War of 1812. Pearl St, on the original shoreline of the East River, was replaced with landfill by Water St, then Front St, and finally South St, where by the 1820s a thick forest of masts congested the port. The **South Street Seaport Museum**.

15

VARIABLE V. GEOGRAPHIC SCALE.

The map above (pg. 620-621) appeared in Richard Saul Wurman's *NYC/ACCESS* in 1983 (colors have been enhanced for clarity), combining a diagrammatic vocabulary—a 30/60/90 degree angle grid—at geographic scale overall. The success of this map, in my opinion is mixed, although Vignelli is quoted in the book, offering a wonderful bit of design history and a cautionary tale of the bureaucratic process:

Originally the design of a New York subway map was part of a comprehensive project ... Three maps were designed: one abstract, for the entire system; one geographical, which showed the actual position of the stations in the context of the area; and one which explained how to get there verbally ... Of this original information network, only the abstract system map was issued for use. That map, like the one in use in London since 1931, was organized on a 45/90 degree angle grid. That configuration has worked well in London ... but obviously did not please all New Yorkers. Although praised for its elegance and design, the map's distortions proved to be difficult for users to understand.

After several years of use, the abstract map was replaced by a new one (although it would have been better to correct the faults of one map, rather than re-educate readers to another). With water in blue and parks in green [see pages 50–51], the present map may be clearer in some instances but, in toto, is a disappointing solution.

The NYC/ACCESS subway map represents the kind of solution we would have wanted to see as a follow-up to our map, rather than the disappointing version we are now offered by the MTA.

The difference between the 2 maps reveals the difficulties of assessing success and failure. One can, of course, make educated guesses based on one's own experience and an understanding of human factors, but user feedback is the ultimate determinant.

The sections of the 2 maps above show the same area of the subway system in rectangles of virtually identical area, centered on Central Park. Overall, the Wurman map is relatively tall and thin while the Vignelli map has squarer proportions. The value of the comparison is compromised by the Wurman map showing trackage while the Vignelli map shows routes (see pages 180–181), which constrains space for larger type (Vignelli likes small type, anyway). The Wurman map, by being geographically accurate, shows true distances as well as the geographic relationship of stations and, therefore, of the city above, including the true proportions of Central Park. This might be appreciated by many users who would equate those relationships to travel and to pedestrian time/distance.

We discussed on pages 161 and 171–173 that we apply appropriate units of measurement to different modes and different scales of the movement experience. For the subway, the unit of measure is the stop rather than feet or miles. So, while the 1983 Wurman map may not retain all the advantages of the 1972 Vignelli map, it does address some of its failings as perceived by users, and it represents a fertile field for discussion.

The above text is taken from:
Designing Information: Human Factors and Common Sense in Information Desin, Joel Katz : Wiley

evokes that era of sea power. By 1812, lawyers, insurance companies, merchants and financiers were crowding out the families in the Financial District, whose symbolic and geographic center became the intersection of Broad and Wall Sts (so called because of the wooden wall that was the northern fortification of *Nieuw Amsterdam*). The construction of the new **Merchants' Exchange** in 1836 speeded up the area's transition to a commercial district.

Today you can visit the current commodities and stock exchanges, but in the limestone-and-glass caverns of Wall St only a few of the old public buildings remain: **Federal Hall**, the former **US Custom House** on Bowling Green, the famous **Trinity Church** (an 1846 incarnation, several times removed from the original), and the less well-known but earlier **St. Paul's Chapel**. A 20th-century masterpiece worth going out of your way to look at is the **Woolworth Building**.

Whitehall conjures up Dutch governor **Peter Stuyvesant**'s mansion (renamed by his English replacement), which was on

Lower Manhattan

Whitehall St. **Bowling Green**, a cattle market in Dutch days, and then a green for bowling and recreation at the center of a desirable residential area, is now an egg-shaped park at the foot of Broadway, with new neighbors but with its 1771 fence still intact. And the **Civic Center**—the cluster of old and new government buildings, some handsome, some horrendous, just north of the Financial District—has become the western boundary of Chinatown.

Created by landfill, the present **Battery Park** offers cooling breezes, welcome greenery and a panoramic view of **New York Harbor**. It's the jumping-off spot for the ferries to **Liberty Island, Ellis Island** and **Staten Island**, the best sightseeing buy for close-ups of the *Statue of Liberty* and the New York City skyline. The Observation Deck at the **World Trade Center** can't be beat for an aerial perspective of Manhattan Island and surrounding territory. Nearby, 2 massive developments, **Battery Park City** and the **World Financial Center**, symbolize Lower Manhattan's emergence as the new epicenter of downtown activity.

1 Ellis Island National Monument (1898, Boring & Tilton) On 1 January 1892, when a boat carrying 148 steerage passengers from the SS *Nevada* pulled into the new pier at Ellis Island, **Annie Moore**, a 15-year-old girl from Ireland, stepped ashore and became the first immigrant to set foot on the island. More than 16 million souls followed in her footsteps before it was closed in 1932. In 1907, its peak year, 1,285,349 people were admitted. The original station burned to the ground in 1897, and the present complex of buildings was already decaying during the WWII years when German aliens were imprisoned there. When it finally closed in 1954, vandals moved in and did their best to destroy what was left. In September 1990, after 8 years of restoration (at a cost of $156 million, with much of the funding spearheaded by **Lee Iacocca**), the main building opened as a museum. The fate of the other 32 buildings is undetermined, although plans to turn the hospital (where immigrants with contagious diseases were held) into an international conference center have been discussed.

On Ellis Island:

Ellis Island Museum of Immigration
Visitors can now follow the footsteps of their ancestors upon arrival in America: from the **Baggage Room**, where they dropped off what were often all of their worldly belongings; to

the **Registry Room**, where they underwent 60-second medical and 30-question legal examinations; and on to the **Staircase of Separation**, which led to the ferryboats that transported the immigrants who were granted admittance (98 percent of those who arrived here) to either Manhattan or New Jersey, where they would then catch trains to points farther west. Also on view are exhibitions tracing the immigration experience: *Treasures from Home* contains personal property brought here by immigrants; the *American Immigrant Wall of Honor*, running along the sea wall overlooking the *Statue of Liberty* and the Manhattan skyline, lists the names of more than 200,000 immigrants who passed through Ellis Island. (Another wall is in the making to accommodate the overwhelming response to the museum's call for names.) In the **Oral History Studio** visitors are given the opportunity to listen to immigrants reminisce about their experiences here. The **Ellis Island Family History Center**, scheduled to open in 1992, will provide visitors with computerized access to the records of 17 million immigrants who landed on Ellis Island and other New York ports. *An RSW recommendation.* ◆ Free. Daily 9AM-5PM. Closed 25 Dec. 363.3267. Ferry from Castle Clinton in Battery Park: Fee (combination ticket to the *Statue of Liberty* available) Daily 9AM-4PM. 269.5755

1 Statue of Liberty National Monument (1886, Frédéric Auguste Bartholdi: pedestal, Richard Morris Hunt) Her official name is *Liberty Enlightening the World*. The figure alone (supported by a steel skeleton engineered by **Gustave Eiffel**) is 151ft high, not counting the pedestal, which adds another 89ft. It is a full 30ft taller than the Colossus of Rhodes, one of the Seven Wonders of the Ancient World. It is interesting to note that Bartholdi's orginal idea was to place a statue of a peasant woman holding the Lamp of Progress to Asia at the entrance to the Suez Canal—an idea that was rejected by the sultan of Egypt. When Bartholdi came to the New World from France looking for a site for *Liberty*, he traveled up and down the Eastern Seaboard and as far west as Salt Lake City, but he never for a moment seriously considered any place but Bedloe's Island, which he saw as his ship sailed into New York Harbor.

Bartholdi placed her carefully. As a ship rounds the Narrows between Brooklyn and Staten Island, she first appears on portside, striding forward in a gesture of welcome. Then, as it passes directly in front of her, she is suddenly erect and saluting. It is an optical illusion, but one of the most impressive in the world.

The island, which was renamed **Liberty Island** in 1956, was used as a quarantine station in the early 18th century, and after 1811 was the site of **Fort Wood**, which is the star-shaped structure that forms the pedestal's base. In the years between, it was a popular place for hanging pirates.

Since the statue's restoration (completed 1986), climbing the spiral staircase to its crown is easier than it had been for 100 years, but there are still 171 steps to climb after the 10-story elevator ride. The view is worth the climb, but the panorama on the ground is impressive too, as is the outlook from the promenade around the top of the pedestal, just under Miss Liberty's feet. The line to go up to the crown can be quite long. You may be turned away if you arrive after 2PM, so plan to visit in the morning. ◆ Liberty Island

Within the *Statue of Liberty*:

The Statue of Liberty Museum
Chronicles the panorama of immigration beginning with the arrival of the Dutch. The museum also contains exhibitions on the statue itself, including the torch, which was re-created and replaced during the 1986 restoration. ◆ Free. Daily 9AM-5PM. 363.3200. Ferry service is from Castle Clinton in Battery Park; frequency varies according to season. Fee. Daily 8:30AM-5PM. 269.5755

2 Battery Park The Dutch began rearranging the terrain the moment **Peter Minuit** bought Manhattan from the Indians in 1626. When they dug their canals and leveled the hills, they dumped the dirt and rocks into the bay. Over the next 300 years or so, more than 21 acres were added to the tip of the island, creating a green buffer between the harbor and the dark canyons of the Financial District. The park takes its name from a line of cannons that once overlooked the harbor. Despite its bellicose name, it has always been a place for those **Herman Melville** described as *...men fixed in ocean reveries.* ◆ Southern tip of Manhattan

Lower Manhattan

Within Battery Park:

Staten Island Ferry This must-do trip for visitors provides an excellent visual orientation to New York City. The ferry leaves from the southern tip of Manhattan, weaves through harbor traffic—from tug to sailboat, yacht to cruise ship—and travels past the *Statue of Liberty* and Ellis Island to the NE edge of Staten Island, then back again. En route, passengers have a glorious view of the city's celebrated skyline. The price, although recently doubled to 50 cents, is still one of the great bargains of our day! ◆ South St at State St

R. O. Blechman

16

17

Illustration R.O. Blechman

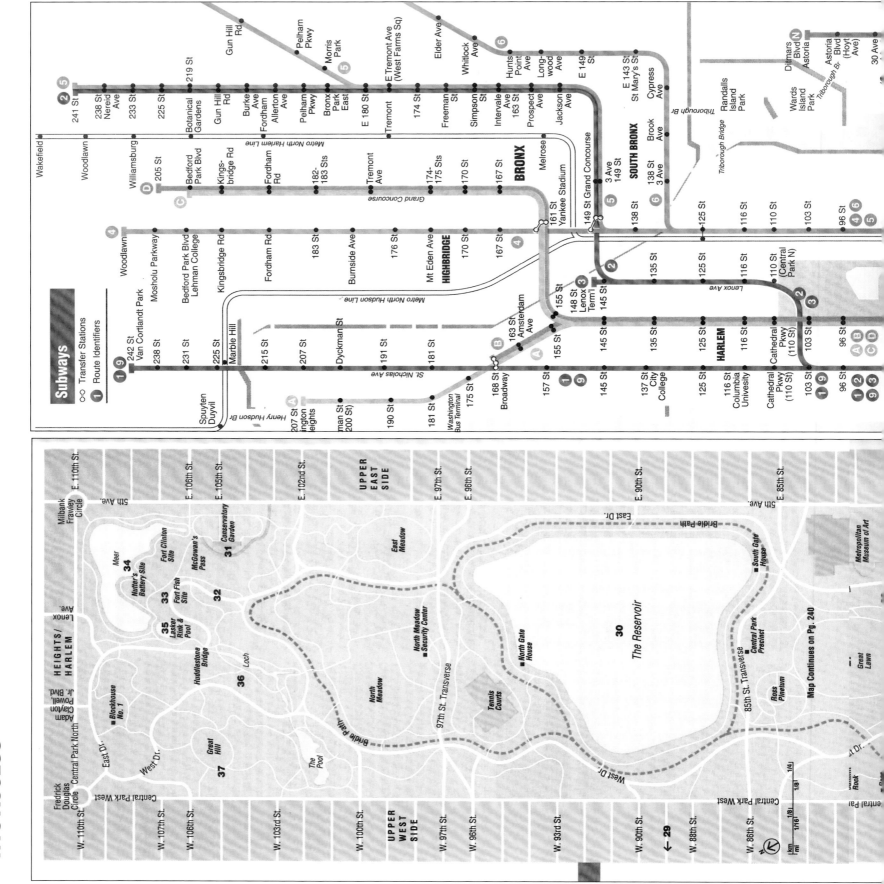

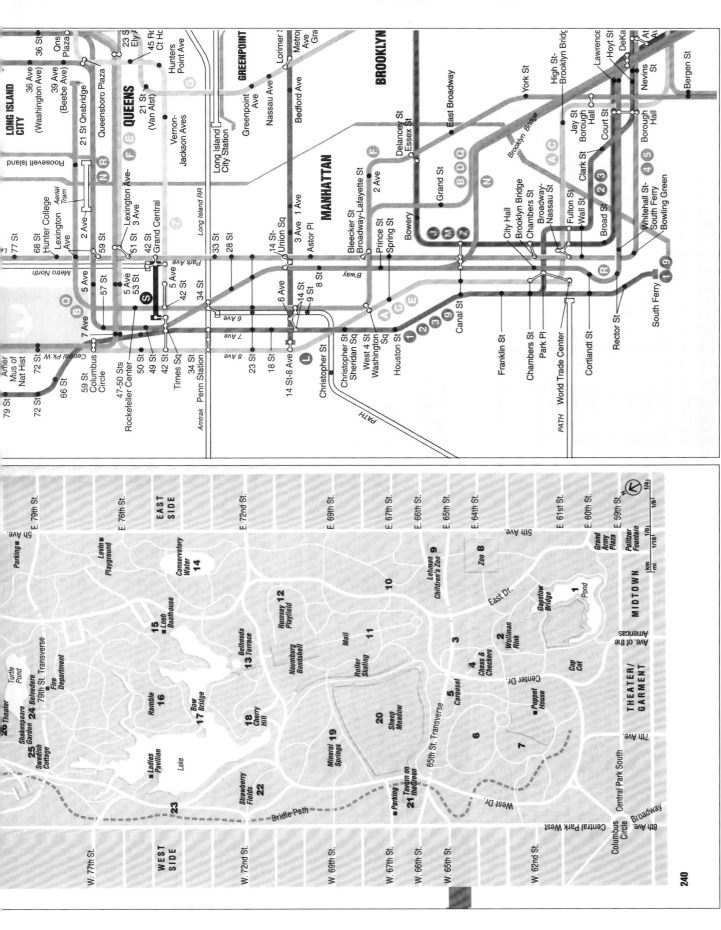

New York City Subway Map Richard Saul Wurman

Central Park Map

51

240

Tokyo is the world's largest department store.

Its aisles
are the subways and highways,
filled with twice as many taxis and people
as New York City.

Its warehouse is the port and the markets.

Its business card is the multiple signature
found in its neon skyline.

Its jewelry department is the mechanical
necklace created by the Yamanote line.

It is a new city in an old location.

It is a new city reborn after disasters,
fiercely preserving the dignity of its past.

It is a young city and a city for the young.
Everything works.

It is uniquely safe in a world of cities filled
with fear.

It is inventive graphically and electronically.

It is perhaps the most expansive and most
expensive of cities.

It is a labyrinth of unmarked, unaddressed
streets where maps to everything are a
necessity and 3 conversations are needed
to find a specific destination.

This bi-lingual book is truly an international
guide both for its intended audience and
throughout its creation both in Japan and
the U.S.
Each page has listings that are near or
next to each other.
Each page is a word map of selected
restaurants, hotels, shops, museums and
architecture.
We have magically placed a blotter paper
of our own invention on 9 areas of this
electronic city to form the pages of this
book.

Jointly developed by C. Itoh Fashion
System Co., Ltd. in Tokyo and
ACCESSPRESS Ltd. in Los Angeles, this
book is intended to bridge the ocean
between resident and tourist.

Our audience for previous books in the
ACCESS series has been divided equally
between those who live in a particular city
and those who choose to visit.

We hope that you find serendipitous
discoveries as you browse through the
pages of **TOKYO**ACCESS

Tokyo is a world city, a world store, a
world factory.

Tokyo is a look at the world 2 years
from now.

RSW

*The Imperial Palace is
used as an orienting element
in the maps throughout this book.*

2.5 kilometers
2500 meters
8200 feet
1.55 miles

3.53 kilometers
3535 meters
11,600 feet
2.2 miles

10 kilometers
10,000 meters
32,800 feet
6.2 miles

東京は世界最大のデパートだ。
たとえばデパートの通路は、地下鉄と首都高
速道路。ニューヨークの２倍の人波とタクシ
ーで埋まっている。
たとえばデパートの倉庫は、東京港と卸売り
市場。

たとえば各売り場の表示は、夜空にきらめく
ネオン。
たとえば宝石売り場は、山手線が作りだすメ
カニカルなネックレスだ。
東京は由緒ある地に生まれた新しい感覚の都
会。破壊のあとに復興の強い情熱により新し
く甦った街だ。
若い都市であり、若ものたちの街でもある。
すべてが躍動している。
でも、恐怖が渦巻いている世界中の都市の中
にあって、驚くほど安全な街でもある。
デザイン面でも先端技術の面でも、常に新し
いものを創り出す都会だ。
たぶん、最も拡がり（エクスパンシブ）があ
り、最も物価の高い（エクスペンシブ）都市
のひとつだろう。
外国人にとって東京は、表示もアドレスも不
明確で迷路のように入り組んだところ。目的
地にたどり着くには、地図と最低３回の会話
を必要とする。
●この２ヵ国語で構成された東京アクセスは、
東京の伊藤忠ファッションシステムとロスア
ンジェルスのアクセス・プレス社との共同編
集によって作られたインターナショナルなガ
イドブックです。
各ページは実際の街並みに沿って、特に選ば
れたレストランやホテル、ショップ、美術館、
建築物などの項目が順序よく並んでいます。
編集にあたっては、エレクトロニクス・シテ
ィ東京を９の地域にわけるため、私たちが開
発した魔法の吸い取り紙を東京の上にかぶせ
ました。東京アクセスは東京人と日本を訪れ
る旅行者の間を隔てる太平洋に架けられた橋
でもあります。これまでのアクセス・シリー
ズも、常にその都市に住む人々と訪れる人々
の両者を読者としてきました。本誌のページ
の中から新しい価値ある発見をされることを
期待しています。
東京は世界の都市であり、世界の店であり、
世界の工場です。２年後の世界を予見させる
都市でもあります。

リチャード・ソール・ワーマン

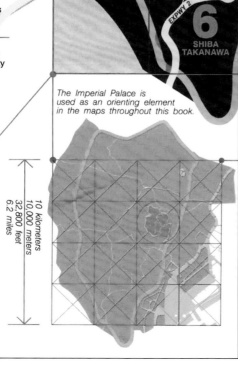

San Francisco at the same scale.

*New York City
(Manhattan Island)
at the same scale.*

Tokyo Bay

TOKYO HOTELS
District entry numbers are in red.

PALACE
13	Palace Hotel	211-5211
24	Tokyo Capital Tokyu Hotel	581-4511
26	Akasaka Tokyu Hotel	580-2311
31	Hotel New Otani	265-1111
32	Akasaka Prince Hotel, New Building	234-1111
32	Akasaka Prince Hotel, Old Building	262-3309
42	Fairmont Hotel	262-1151
51	Hotel Grand Palace	264-1111

MARUNOUCHI
8	Tokyo Marunouchi Hotel	215-2151
12	Tokyo Station Hotel	231-2511

GINZA
3	Imperial Hotel	504-1111
11	Shinbashi Daiichi Hotel	501-4411
15	Ginza Nikko Hotel	571-4911
95	Mitsui Urban Hotel Ginza	572-4131
96	Ginza Dai-Ichi Hotel	542-5311
101	Ginza Tokyu Hotel	541-2411
116	Ginza Marunouchi Hotel	543-5431
127	Ginza Capital Hotel	543-8211
135	Yaesu Fujiya Hotel	273-2111
159	Holiday Inn Tokyo	553-6161

SHIBUYA
12	Shibuya Tobu Hotel	476-0111
23	Hillport Hotel	462-5171
30	Shibuya Tokyu Inn	498-0109
48	President Hotel	497-0111

AKASAKA/ROPPONGI
1	Hotel Okura	582-0111
25	Akasaka Shanpia Hotel	586-0811
26	Asia Center of Japan	402-6111
38	Hotel Ibis	403-4411
67	Roppongi Prince Hotel	587-1111

SHIBA/TAKANAWA
1	Shinagawa Prince Hotel	440-1111
2	Hotel Pacific Tokyo	445-6711
3	New Takanawa Prince Hotel	442-1111
4	Takanawa Prince Hotel	447-1111
11	Miyako Hotel	447-3111
19	Tokyo Prince Hotel	432-1111
23	Shiba Park Hotel	433-4141
31	Atagoyama Tokyu Inn	431-0109

SHINJUKU
10	Keio Plaza Hotel	344-0111
14	Century Hyatt Tokyo	349-0111
15	Tokyo Hilton International	344-5111
16	Shinjuku Washington Hotel	343-3111
44	Shinjuku Prince Hotel	205-1111
67	Tokyo International Youth Hostel	235-1107

UENO/DOWNTOWN
16	Suigetsu Hotel/Ogai-ko	822-4611
63	Ryokan Mikawaya Bekkan	843-2345
98	Tokyo YMCA Hotel	293-1911
119	Hilltop Hotel	293-2311

IKEBUKURO
4	Sunshine City Prince Hotel	988-1111

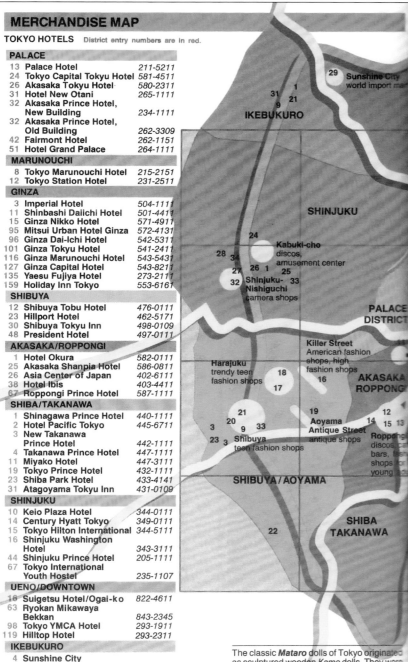

The Metropolitan Central Wholesale Market was established in 1935 to ensure price-controlled processing and distribution of perishables in the city. Today, the Central Wholesale Market is split into 12 major and 7 minor outlets serving the entire metro area. The fruits, vegetables, meat and seafood processed here are distributed throughout eastern Japan. Deliveries from shipping organizations in production centers consigned by wholesalers are auctioned off to retailers, restaurateurs and large consumer organizations. The items finally reach the individual consumer either directly or through these middlemen.

The classic **Mataro** dolls of Tokyo originated as sculptured wooden **Kamo** dolls. They were created in Kyoto during the 18th century. These dolls were swathed in leftover fabrics from Shinto priests' robes; made of young willow, the unpolished texture gave the dolls' skin a pronounced greenish tint. The first **Kimekomi** dolls in **Edo** were brought over from Kyoto as gifts. Later during the Meiji era, a famous dollmaker by the name of **Eikichi Yoshino** invented a new method of molding the base form of a doll from fine sawdust mixed with glue. This method made it possible to reproduce the same doll in limited quantities, making them available to more people. Through Eikichi's son, the process has since been handed down to **Mataro Kanabayashi,** who has perfected the doll-making technique of today.

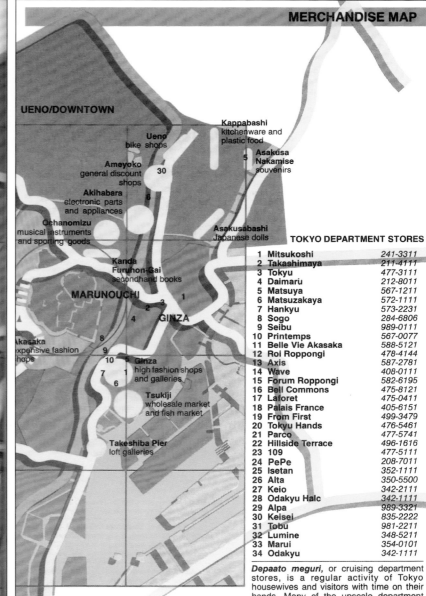

TOKYO DEPARTMENT STORES
1	Mitsukoshi	241-3311
2	Takashimaya	211-4111
3	Tokyu	477-3111
4	Daimaru	212-8011
5	Matsuya	567-1211
6	Matsuzakaya	572-1111
7	Hankyu	573-2231
8	Sogo	284-6806
9	Seibu	989-0111
10	Printemps	567-0077
11	Belle Vie Akasaka	588-5121
12	Roi Roppongi	478-4144
13	Axis	587-2781
14	Wave	408-0111
15	Forum Roppongi	582-6195
16	Bell Commons	475-8121
17	Laforet	475-0411
18	Palais France	405-6151
19	From First	499-3479
20	Tokyu Hands	476-5461
21	Parco	477-5741
22	Hillside Terrace	496-1616
23	109	477-5111
24	PePe	208-7011
25	Isetan	352-1111
26	Alta	350-5500
27	Keio	342-2111
28	Odakyu Halc	342-1111
29	Alpa	989-3321
30	Keisei	835-2222
31	Tobu	981-2211
32	Lumine	348-5211
33	Marui	354-0101
34	Odakyu	342-1111

Furoshiki, the Japanese wrapping cloth used to wrap everything from gifts to garbage, is the oldest of all Japanese textile articles, even older than the **kimono.** Dating back to the 8th century, the earliest furoshiki (bath sheets) were used to dry off the noblemen who frequented the first public bath houses in Japan. During the **Edo** era, the prospering merchant classes used furoshiki to deliver individual consumer goods. Different furoshiki designs are used for different occasions: the crane, symbol of longevity, is the pattern for wedding gift wraps; purple, the color of nobility, is popular for more solemn occasions. In recent years, department stores have emblazoned furoshiki with hot colors and punk-rock images. Attempting to introduce the furoshiki to Japanese teenagers, who dismiss it as old-fashioned, the textile industry is now commissioning young designers to create a new craze for the beautiful, reusable wrap.

Depaato meguri, or cruising department stores, is a regular activity of Tokyo housewives and visitors with time on their hands. Many of the upscale department stores feature not only departments with fashion and houseware merchandise, but also hold adult classes in such diverse topics as **ikebana,** calligraphy and computer programming. Part of the fun at these giant shopping palaces is the exhibition area. More than one million people came to Takashimaya's Nihonbashi store in 1983 just to see the Columbia space shuttle.

Food products are another boon to department stores, with entire floors devoted to luscious edibles from local and foreign markets. Pre-packaged and fresh foods account for about 20 percent of total sales, and it has been estimated that a store would lose 30 percent of its clientele without this special section.

To ensure a safe and trouble-free browsing experience for mothers with young children, several stores provide a supervised play room, a separate diaper-changing area, children's dentist and consultants who give parental advice.

TOKYO ACCESS

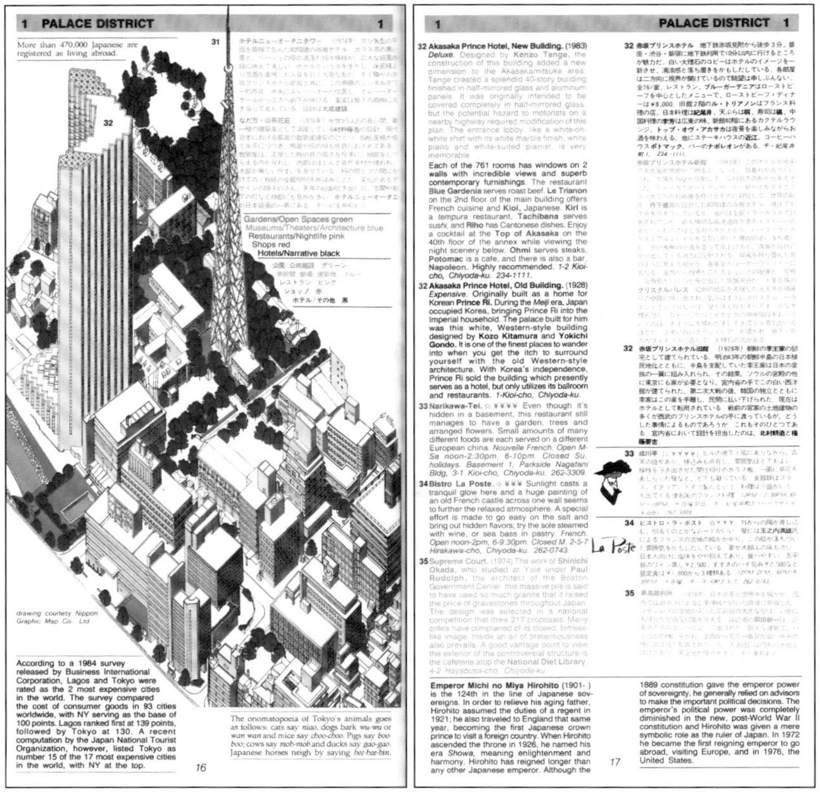

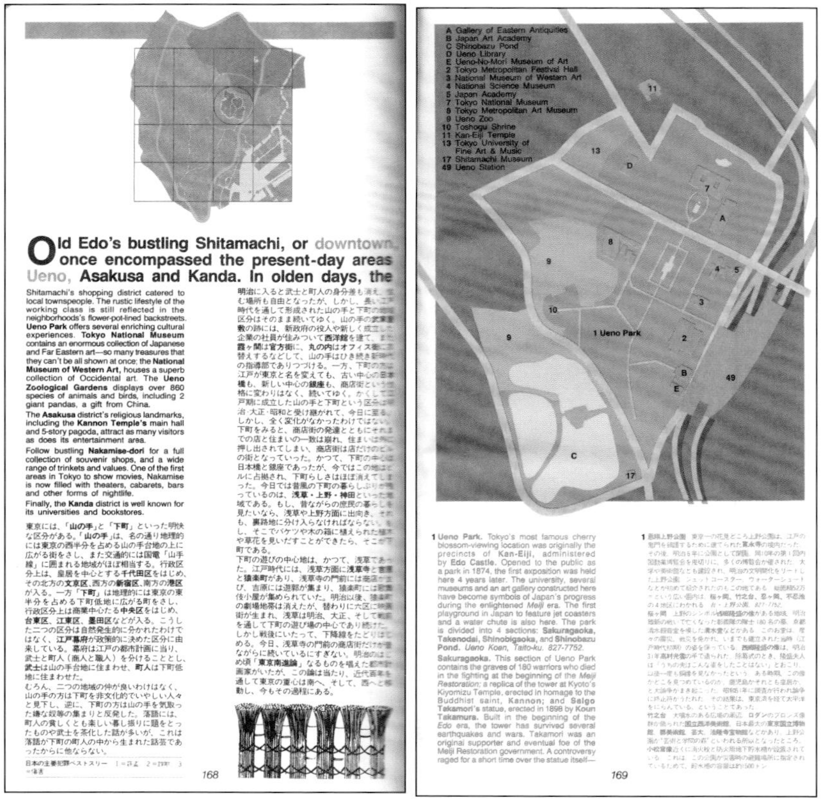

21 Kasumigaseki Building. (1968) Japan's first skyscraper with a height of 147 meters (36 floors) was designed by Yamashita Architects and took a full 6 years to complete. Earthquake requirements prevented any sign of a taller building in 1961, special areas of the city were zoned for high density construction; this building provides a total area 9 times that of the site. The top floor houses an observation gallery. 1-1 Kasumigaseki, Chiyoda-ku.

22 Water Level Bench Mark Repository. (1891) Here is the standard by which elevations throughout the country—mountains, hills and plains—are measured. A quartz plaque inscribed with a red line is mounted on a marble market and set at a point of 80.3 feet (24.5 meters) above the average water level of the Sumisei River. From this point all elevations in the country can be deduced, even the average height of housewives is measured in a small building that lies all the dignity of a Roman temple. Designed by Shichijiro Sasachi, one of the first modern architects of Japan. 1-1 Nagata-cho, Chiyoda-ku.

23 The Diet Building (Parliament). (1936, Yoshikazu Okuma and Kenkichi Yabashi). Called Kokkai-Gijido in Japanese, this Western-style capital building, modeled after statehouses in Europe and the U.S. is very out-of-place in Tokyo. The right wing houses the House of Councillors, formerly limited to the meeting place of the House of Representatives. In the center is a 200-foot high (65 meters) clock tower. The entire mass of gray granite took 16 years to finish. Show your passport at the reception desk for admittance. 1-7 Nagata-cho, Chiyoda-ku.

24 Tokyo Capital Tokyu Hotel. Expensive/deluxe. Located on a hillside beside the Hie Shrine and known as the Tokyo Hilton until December 1983, it is noted for its 479 large rooms, each equipped with wet bar. The hotel's Family Service offers an extra bed for children free of charge, Mr. Muragi, the in-house barber, was General Douglas MacArthur's tonsor during the occupation. Excellent service. Highly recommended.

Also at the hotel are:
Keyaki Grill (☆☆ ¥¥), the hotel's main dining room, serves nouvelle French cuisine. There are also the Origami Corner House tea lounge-garden cafe-coffee shop for snacks, Genji Japanese restaurant, Hoshigaoka Chinese restaurant, and 2 bars: Misao Lounge and Ripo Bar. 2-10-3 Nagata-cho, Chiyoda-ku. 581-4511.

25 Hie Jinja Shrine, also known as Sanno-san, is one of the city's most popular shrines and the site of the mid-June Sanno-sai Festival, one of the largest in the city. The shrine is dedicated to Oyamakuni; statues of the resident monkey god guard the entrance. During the festival, palanquins carrying mikoshi (miniature shrines) are paraded through the neighborhood. Sanno-sama's influence is believed to cement relationships, grant fertility and ward off evil. 2-10-5 Nagata-cho, Chiyoda-ku. 581-2471.

drawing courtesy Nippon Graphic Map Co. Ltd.

12

26 Akasaka Tokyu Hotel. Expensive. Known affectionately as the Pajama Hotel because of the eye-catching candy-striped exterior, the hotel is close to Aoyama's shopping area. The first 3 floors have a wide selection of fashionable boutiques selling famous domestic and international couture, tableware and accessories. Gondola (¥¥¥), the main dining room, serves French cuisine, and offers a 14th-floor view of Tokyo by night. Also at the hotel are a coffee house providing a comprehensive food and drink menu throughout the night, the Bar Gondola with its impressive night view, and the Marco Polo Bar. The Nagaura Soba noodle shop on the Basement 1 level is highly recommended. 2-14-3 Nagata-cho, Chiyoda-ku. 580-2311.

Diet. Late Medieval English from the Medieval Latin word dieta, dieta (way of living). Legislative assembly or administrative council, first important in German history. The German Diet was dissolved in the 1800s, but Japan and many other European nations still use the borrowed term. According to the Japanese constitution, the Diet is the sole law-making organ of the country. Two chambers constitute the Diet: the lower House of Representatives and the upper House of Councillors.

drawing courtesy Nippon Graphic Map Co. Ltd.

13

More than 470,000 Japanese are registered as living abroad.

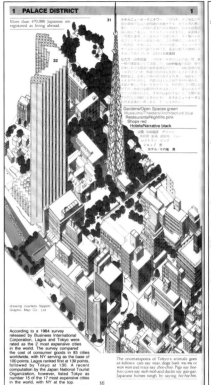

Gardens/Open Spaces green
Museums/Theaters/Architecture blue
Shops red
Hotels/Narrative black

drawing courtesy Nippon Graphic Map Co. Ltd.

According to a 1984 survey released by Business International Corporation, Lagos and Tokyo were rated as the 2 most expensive cities in the world. The survey compared the cost of consumer goods in 93 cities worldwide, with NY serving as the base of 100 points. Lagos ranked first at 139 points, followed by Tokyo at 130. A recent computation by the Japan National Tourist Organization, however, listed Tokyo as number 15 of the 17 most expensive cities in the world, with NY at the top.

The onomatopoeia of Tokyo's animals goes as follows: cats say nian, dogs bark wa-wa or wan wan and mice say choo-choo. Pigs say boo boo; cows say moh-moh and ducks say gaa-gaa. Japanese horses neigh by saying bee-hee-hin.

16

32 Akasaka Prince Hotel, New Building. (1983) Deluxe. Designed by Kenzo Tange, the construction of this building added a new dimension to the Akasaka-mitsuke area. Tange created a splendid 40-story building finished in half-mirrored glass and aluminum panels. It was originally intended to be covered completely in half-mirrored glass, but the potential hazard to motorists on a nearby highway required modification of this plan. The entrance lobby, like a whole-on white marble finish, with piano and white-suited grand piano, is very memorable.

Each of the 761 rooms has windows on 2 walls with incredible views and superb contemporary furnishings. The restaurant Blue Gardenia serves roast beef; Le Trianon on the 2nd floor of the main building offers French cuisine and Kiol, a tempura restaurant; Tachibana serves sushi; and Riho has Cantonese dishes. Enjoy a cocktail at the Top of Akasaka on the 40th floor of the annex while viewing the night scenery below. Ohmi serves steaks; Potomac is a cafe; and there is also a bar, Napoleon. Highly recommended. 1-2 Kioi-cho, Chiyoda-ku. 234-1111.

32 Akasaka Prince Hotel, Old Building. (1928) Expensive. Originally built as a home for Korean Prince Ri. During the Meiji era, Japan occupied Korea, bringing Prince Ri into the imperial household. The palace built for him was this white, Western-style building designed by Kozo Kitamura and Yokichi Gondo. It is one of the finest places to wander into when you get the itch to surround yourself with the old Western-style architecture. With Korea's independence, Prince Ri sold the building which presently serves as a hotel, but only utilizes its ballroom and restaurants. 1-Kioi-cho, Chiyoda-ku.

33 Narikawa-Tei. ☆☆¥¥ Even though it is hidden in a basement, this restaurant still manages to have a garden, trees and arranged flowers. Small amounts of many different foods are each served on a different European china. Nouvelle French. Open M-Sa noon-2:30pm, 6-10pm. Closed Su, holidays. Basement 1, Parkside Nagatani Bldg., 3-1 Kioi-cho, Chiyoda-ku. 262-3309.

33 Bistro La Poste. ☆¥¥¥ Sunlight casts a tranquil glow here and a huge painting of an old French cuisine across one wall seems to further the relaxed atmosphere. A special effort is made to go easy on the salt and bring out hidden flavors; try the sole steamed with wine, or sea bass in pastry. French. Open noon-2pm, 6-9:30pm. Closed M. 2-5-7 Hirakawa-cho, Chiyoda-ku. 262-0743.

35 Supreme Court. (1974) The work of Shinichi Okada, who studied at Yale under Paul Rudolph, the architect of the Boston Government Center, this massive one is said to have used so much granite that it raised the price of gravestones throughout Japan. The design was selected in a national competition that drew 217 proposals. Many residents found the concrete of, closed, fortress-like image. Inside an air of orderlessness also prevails. A good vantage point to view the exterior of the commercial structure is the cafeteria atop the National Diet Library. 4-2 Hayabusa-cho, Chiyoda-ku.

Emperor Michi no Miya Hirohito (1901-) is the 124th in the line of Japanese sovereigns. In order to relieve his aging father, Hirohito assumed the duties of a regent in 1921; he also traveled to England that same year, becoming the first Japanese crown prince to visit a foreign country. When Hirohito ascended the throne in 1926, he named his era Showa, meaning enlightenment and harmony. Hirohito has reigned longer than any other Japanese emperor. Although the 1889 constitution gave the emperor power of sovereignty, he generally relied on advisors to make the important political decisions. The emperor's political power was completely diminished in the new, post-World War II constitution and Hirohito was given a mere symbolic role as the ruler of Japan. In 1972 he became the first reigning emperor to go abroad, visiting Europe, and in 1976, the United States.

17

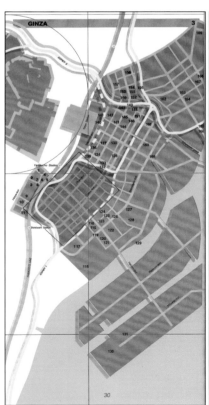

Yurakucho Station

Shinbashi Station

30

1 Sanshin Building. (1929) The exterior is not much to look at, but the indoor arcade is a wonderland. A single passageway runs the length of the building, flanked by boutiques, shops, service (cleaners, beauticians, etc.) and restaurants; the whole way. The star-filled sky overhead is beginning to fade, but the indirect lighting and the art deco motif on the elevator lobby are still striking. An inexplicable light, bright feeling superimposed on old-style elegance. Designed by Tamisuke Yokogawa and Kitaro Matsui. 1-10 Yuraku-cho, Chiyoda-ku.

2 Nissei Hibiya Building (Nissei Theatre). (1963) Designed by Togo Murano and built in the 1960s as a reaction to its contemporaries' angular concentration upon functionalism at all costs. The granite walls, balcony windows and massive columns of this building seem to express the personality of the architect. The ceiling in the theater is flecked with pieces of mother-of-pearl and the walls are finished in glass mosaic. Lights flaming between the walls and ceiling create the impression of underwater world. The marble floor and the art deco ceiling of the lobby are another indication of the architect's disregard for the conventions of his time. 1-1-1 Yuraku-cho, Chiyoda-ku.

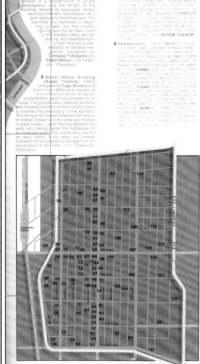

Old Edo's bustling Shitamachi, or downtown, once encompassed the present-day areas Ueno, Asakusa and Kanda. In olden days, the

Shitamachi's shopping district catered to local townspeople. The rustic lifestyle of the working class is still reflected in the neighborhoods's flower-pot-lined backstreets. Ueno Park offers several enriching cultural experiences. Tokyo National Museum contains an extensive collection of Japanese and Far-Eastern art—so many treasures that they can't be all shown at once; the National Museum of Western Art, houses a superb collection of Occidental art. The Ueno Zoological Gardens displays over 860 species of animals and birds, including 2 giant pandas, a gift from China.

The Asakusa district's religious landmarks, including the Kannon Temple's main hall and 5-story pagoda, attract as many visitors as does its entertainment area.

Follow bustling Nakamise-dori for a full collection of souvenir shops, and a wide range of trinkets and values. One of the first areas in Tokyo to show movies, Nakamise is now filled with theaters, cabarets, bars and other forms of nightlife.

Finally, the Kanda district is well known for its universities and bookstores.

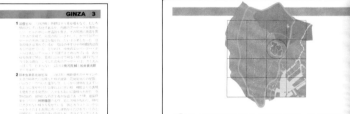

168

A Gallery of Eastern Antiquities
B Japan Art Academy
C Ueno Library
D Shinobazu Pond
1 Ueno-No-Mori Museum of Art
2 Tokyo Metropolitan Festival Hall
3 National Museum of Western Art
4 National Science Museum
5 Japan Academy
6 Tokyo National Museum
7 Tokyo Metropolitan Art Museum
8 Ueno Zoo
10 Toshogu Shrine
11 Kan-Eiji Temple
12 Tokyo University of Fine Art & Music
14 Shitamachi Museum
49 Ueno Station

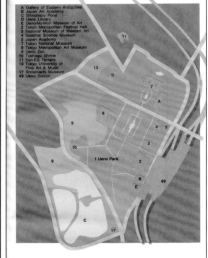

1 Ueno Park

1 Ueno Park. Tokyo's most famous cherry blossom-viewing location was originally the precincts of Kan-Eiji, administered by Edo Castle. Opened to the public as a park in 1874, the first exposition was held here 4 years later. The university, several museums and an art gallery constructed here have become symbols of Japan's progress during the enlightened Meiji era. The first playground in Japan to feature a roller coaster and a water chute is also here. The park is divided into 4 sections: Sakuragaoka, Tokenodai, Shinobazuoka, and Shitamachi Pond. Ueno Koen, Taito-ku. 827-7752.

Sakuragaoka. This section of Ueno Park contains the graves of 180 warriors who died in the fighting at the beginning of the Meiji Restoration; a replica of the tower at Kyoto's Kiyomizu Temple, erected in homage to the Buddhist saint, Kannon; and Saigo Takamori's statue, erected in 1898 by Koun Takamura. Built in the beginning of the Edo era, the tower has survived several earthquakes and wars. Takamori was an original supporter and eventual foe of the Meiji Restoration government. A controversy raged for a short time over the statue itself—

169

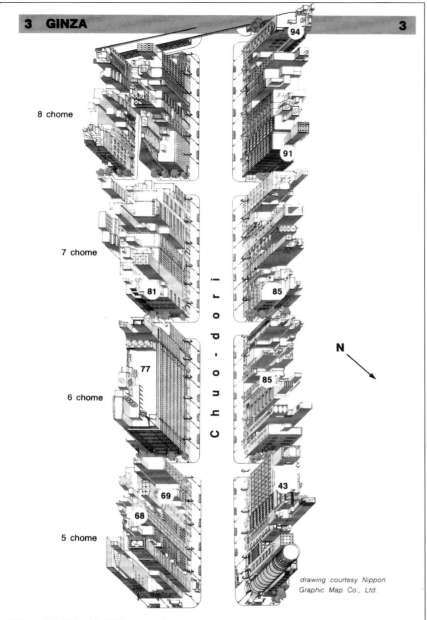

8 chome

7 chome

6 chome

5 chome

81

77

69

68

94

91

85

85

43

C h u o - d o r i

N

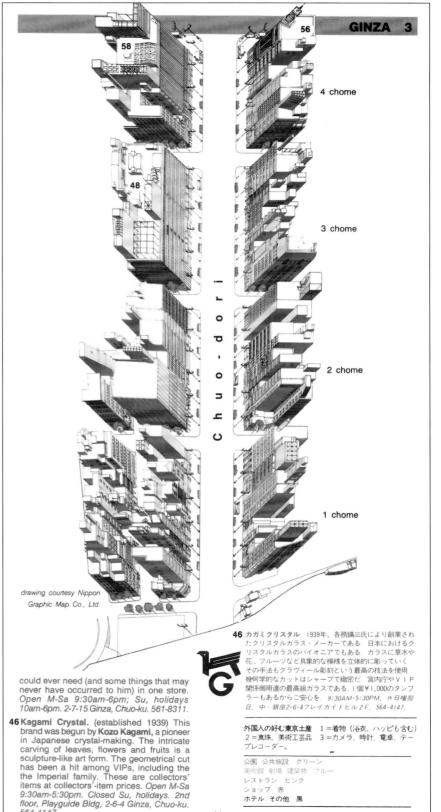

56

58

48

4 chome

3 chome

2 chome

1 chome

C h u o - d o r i

drawing courtesy Nippon Graphic Map Co., Ltd.

drawing courtesy Nippon Graphic Map Co., Ltd.

45 Itoya. Established in 1904 as a stationery store, this is a favorite stop for everyone, from kids looking for crayons to professional designers and draftsmen. A quick rundown on their stock gives us the following list: **Basement 1**—typewriters, rubber stamps; **Basement 2**—wrapping paper, gift boxes, notes; **1st floor**—cards and fashionable notepaper; **Mezzanine**—fountain pens, desk accessories, quality stationery; **2nd floor**—files, ballpoint pens, office supplies; **3rd floor**—desks, lighting, file cabinets; **4th floor**—hobby floor stocking computer games, radio-controlled models, games; **5th floor**—paper goods, both Japanese and imported, and a selection of wallpaper; **6th floor**—art and graphic design products; **7th floor**—press type, offset printing service, color copies; **8th floor**—picture frames and framing service; **9th floor**—tearoom and **gallery** exhibiting the works of different illustrators every week. Anything the artist

45 伊東屋 和洋文房具店として、1904年（明治37年）の創業である　子供からプロのデザイナーまで、様々な客で店内はいつもにぎわっている。では、各フロア毎の売り場構成を説明しよう。地下は、タイプライター、印刷関連、印章　中地下は包装紙、ギフトボックス、ノートなど点数も豊富にある　1階はカート、ノートなどのファンシー商品のフロア　ここはいつも女の子や子供であふれている　中2階は万年筆やさいふなど高級ステイショーナリー　2階には、ファイル、ボールペンなど事務用品がすべて揃う　3階は机、照明などインテリア用品　4階はホビーフロアー　パソコンやラジコン、ゲーム類がある。5階は和洋紙各種　壁紙も種類が多い　6階は画材、デザイン用品のフロアー　7階は、文字と加工サービス。オフセット印刷やカラーコピーも出来る。8階は額縁絵全般。特注も受けている　そして9階はティーラウンジとギャラリーとなっている　1週間単位で催しものが変わり、特に若手イラストレーターの作品展などに人気がある。以上、文房具に関してないものはないという店である。　入口横の歩道上でアイティア商品の説明即売会が開かれるが、これがまた伊東屋訪問の楽しみの一つとなる。　9:30AM-6PM（平日）、10AM-6PM（日曜祭日）、休無休、中・銀座2-7-15、561-8311.

could ever need (and some things that may never have occurred to him) in one store. *Open M-Sa 9:30am-6pm; Su, holidays 10am-6pm. 2-7-15 Ginza, Chuo-ku. 561-8311.*

46 Kagami Crystal. (established 1939) This brand was begun by **Kozo Kagami,** a pioneer in Japanese crystal-making. The intricate carving of leaves, flowers and fruits is a sculpture-like art form. The geometrical cut has been a hit among VIPs, including the the Imperial family. These are collectors'-item prices. *Open M-Sa 9:30am-5:30pm. Closed Su, holidays. 2nd floor, Playguide Bldg, 2-6-4 Ginza, Chuo-ku. 564-4147.*

46 カガミクリスタル 1939年、各務鑛三氏により創業されたクリスタルガラス・メーカーである　日本におけるクリスタルガラスのパイオニアでもある　ガラスに草木や花、フルーツなど具象的な模様を立体的に彫っていくその手法もグラヴィール彫刻という最高の技法を使用　幾何学的なカットはシャープで緻密だ。宮内庁やVIP関係御用達の最高級ガラスである　1個¥1,000のタンブラーもあるからご安心を　9:30AM-5:30PM、休日曜祭日、中・銀座2-6-4プレイガイドビル2F、564-4147.

外国人の好む東京土産　1＝着物（浴衣、ハッピも含む）　2＝真珠、美術工芸品　3＝カメラ、時計、電卓、テープレコーダー。

公園　公共施設　グリーン
美術館　劇場　建築物　ブルー
レストラン　ピンク
ショップ　赤
ホテル／その他　黒

40

41

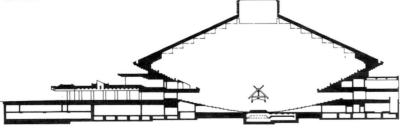

Tadanori Yokoo

Tadanori Yokoo

85 New Kokugikan. (1984) Designed as the new center for *Sumo* wrestling, this building on the banks of the Sumida River is an excellent fusion of modern and traditional forms. Since Sumo is performed here only 45 days each year (other matches are held in alternating areas of the country), the earthen ring required for Sumo can be removed to provide room for other sports. The building also houses the **Sumo Museum** (see below) and other facilities which are open to the public. It was designed by **Kajima Construction** and **Takashi Sugiyama** design offices. *1-20 Yokoami, Sumida-ku.*

85 Sumo Museum. On the grounds of the new Kokugikan, this museum contains a large collection of *sumo* memorabilia, trophies, books, photographs, and ancient prints related to the sport. Open January 1985. *Open M-F. Closed Sa, Su, holidays and New Year's holidays. 1-20 Yokoami, Sumida-ku. 851-2206.*

85 新国技館 （1984年）両国の地に、再び国技館が帰ってきた。四周が切られた方形の屋根と聳え立つ大屋根が、格調高い 趣味の造型」を感じさせる。くるりと河川を表象に取り込まれた中央に、可動する土俵のある。この近代的でも均衡の相撲が見られるのは、年 3回、45日である他の日には、土俵を下げ、一括網取も移動させて、レスリング、ボクシング、柔剣道場として利用出来る 相撲博物館、相撲教習所、相撲診療所も設けられており、一町によっ望されている 鹿島建設建築設計本部。 杉山隆建築設計事務所の共同設計　景：像別・20。

85 相撲博物館 同上に新装した国技館の敷地内にある約3700点、遺品・記念品560点、古書500点。写真6000点の資料を収蔵し、これらを展示して相撲の世界を伝えている 見どころは日本書紀にも記された相撲の神様、野見宿禰力のレタートルほどの面、ダイヤモルヒーを財りはめた常陸山の豪華な化粧廻し、全財圧、相撲、相撲大全などの古文書 平安朝相撲節会の図、元禄相撲の勝など飾りたくさん 相撲ファンならずともたいっぱ楽しめる 新国技館の誕生にともなう 昭和60年からオープンする、光80年v4あせは、ここは土俵や 年 あたらは、相撲いっぱいちゅうじゅう、運が、手・単数、明の

Kajima Corporation and Takashi Sugiyama

According to regulations, a **sumo wrestler** should weigh at least 165 pounds.

There are 105 memberships in the **Japan Sumo Association**, each priced at over $20,000.

Sumo or classical wrestling, goes back to the 8th-century autumn festival of *Nara*. Six championships are held annually, 3 of which take place in Tokyo's *Kokugikan* in mid-January, mid-May and September. The giant wrestlers—their size is attributed to gland problems and constant overeating—range from 5-feet 8 inch, 230-pounders to 6-foot 2 inch, 345-pound mastodons. Not all sumo wrestlers are Japanese: former sumo wrestler **Takamiyama** is from Hawaii; **Maenoyama** is Korean; **Taiho,** the superman who retired in 1971, is half-Russian. A sumo wrestler's day begins with a rigorous workout from 5am until noontime. Then, after a soothing bath, the athlete sits down to his main meal of boiled meat and vegetables, steaks and unlimited quantities of rice. Afternoons are spent napping and then! it's time for the big bang. The champion bouts are televised, complete with enthusiastic commentators and instant replays. Incorrect starts occur; the sullen champions waddle back to the sand-covered ring, where they crouch until the referee signals with a fan to attack. The earthshaking encounter is over in less than a minute. Hand or body-pushing and thrusting is done in 70 different ways, with the loser being forced outside the 15-footcircle or pinned to the ground. Afterwards, winner and loser bow face-to-face and exit to collect their bounty. The Grand Champion gets a very generous monthly allowance from the sumo guild, plus gifts from his loving fans—which brings his salary above the ¥1 million-mark per month.

The use of **bamboo swords** in *kendo* was introduced in the late 18th century.

Kendo (way of the sword) originated as fencing with a 2-hand sword during the Sui dynasty (589-618) in China. In the late 12th century, the long-bladed weapon was brought over to Japan's capital, *Kamakura,* where the rising class of martial aristocrats—the *samurai*—adopted the sword skill as *kenjutsu* or *gekken.* From this time until the Tokugawa Shogunate's rise to power in the 17th century, *kenjutsu* was practiced through *kata,* formal attack exercises carried out with a training sword made of oak. After a decline of 2 centuries, kenjutsu was renamed *kendo* and installed as a regular course in Japanese schools in the early 1900s.

The weapon used in kendo is made of 4 shafts of split bamboo held together by a silk or nylon cord twisted 3 times around the leather grip. The length of the sword varies: for junior high school students it is 3.7 feet long, for high school students 3.8 feet. Adults fence with a sword no less than 3.9 feet in length. The protection equipment consists of a face mask (*men*), pulled over a cotton towel which is tied to the head by 2 cords. A breastplate (*do*) protects the chest. Five thick panels of fabric protect the thighs; the same quilted material is also used in the padded mittens (*kote*). Training usually entails diffferent attack and defense movements called *waza.* Free-style is the common practice, where stance, footwork, cuts, thrusts, feints, and parries are repeated over and over (*kakari keiko*). Points in the 5-minute matches are scored by cuts, either to the center of the head, to the temple, either side of the trunk, or cuts to the wrists at waist level. The thrusts are accompanied by calls telling onlookers exactly where the sword hit.

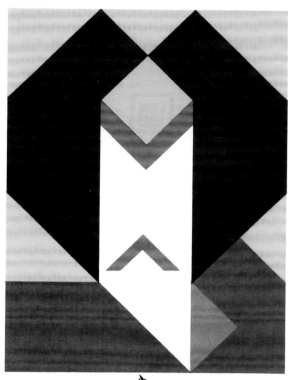

Ikko Tanaka

Ikko Tanaka

111 Ginno-To Hirai (☆ ¥) serves beef stew and shrimp gratin only. The gratin is available in portions for 2 or more. *Open W-M noon-8pm. Closed Tu. 4-13-6 Ginza, Chuo-ku. 541-6395.*

112 Magazine House. (1983) Striped by countless glinting pink and silver tiles, Magazine House presents a *colorful* picture. The building, designed by **Teiichi Takahashi,** is headquarters for a Tokyo publishing house producing youth culture magazines such as **Brutus.** One is greeted at the entrance by **Popeye** and **Olive** figures, namesakes of 2 other House publications and, once inside, some unusual lighting takes effect. The lobby's ceiling is lined with rows of frosted bulbs encased in old-fashioned frilled glass shades. Everything glitters, walls included. To the left is a video room, its elevated glass roof overlooked by a metal pipe-shaped balcony for a high-tech effect. The **World Magazine Library**, at the head of the main stairway, contains what seems to be every magazine in the world—an ideal place to browse for a few hours. Really worth a visit to see this extraordinary array of print material. *3-13-10 Ginza, Chuo-ku.*

113 Okumura Shoten. A professional drama/*Kabuki* bookstore, Okumura's is frequented by set designers, wig stylists, costume specialists, etc. Most of the drama books are too technical for amateurs. Nothing is available in English. Light reading has been added near the door for the business crowd. *Open M-Sa 10am-7pm. Closed Su, holidays. 3-9-2 Ginza, Chuo-ku. 543-3604.*

Women constitute 38 percent of the labor force in Japan.

公園 公共施設 グリーン
美術館 劇場 建築物 ブルー
レストラン ピンク
ショップ 赤
ホテル/その他 黒

111 銀の塔ひら井 ☆ ¥ ビーフシチューとエビグラタンだけの店だが、初めての人はメニューがないのでとまどうことだろう グラタンは2人前から受けつける *12AM-8PM.* 休火曜. 中・銀座4-13-6. 541-6395.

112 マガジンハウス （1983年）キラキラ光るメタリックなタイルを全身にまとっている 銀座の地にピンクのストライフが冴やかで 若者向けの雑誌を発行している出版社の本社ビル 設計は第一工房（高橋靖一）揺さのタイトルでもある「ポパイ」と「オリーブ」が出迎えてくれる 玄関を入ると、ロビー内部があやしい光に満ちている 戦後、バラック住宅の屋根でよく見かけたトタンに特殊加工を施し、銀色に光らせて天井や壁に使っているのだ 左手階段を数段上がると、カラス屋根の大吹き抜けをもつビデオルーム 上部空間は全線の綱を思わせるバルコニーや、吹き出し口のハイフが飛びだし、ハイテックな小さな電球がおさまって天井一面に並んでいる 時代の先端をいく外観のビルに、トタンやカラスの笠という、日本が貧しかった頃にはどこでも見かけた部材をも意識したデザインの この空間とロビーの境にある無地の大理石のベンチに腰をおろすと、ゆったりした気分を味わうことが出来る 正面階段上のワールド・マガジンギャラリーには世界の雑誌が集まる 少々ところが寂しい時に半日ほど過ごすには絶好の穴場 ロビーの天井に目を向けると、昔風のフリルかついたカラスの笠に、小さな電球がおさまって天井一面に並んでいる 中・銀座3-13-10.

113 奥村書店 歌舞伎・演劇書の専門店である 演劇人や舞台の衣裳・かつら・大道具・小道具関係の人、文筆家などその道の専門家が多く来る店だ 外人客もたまに来るが、英文の書は現在、置いてない それに、内容がかなり専門的なものが多いため、ちょっと玄人に興味ある専門的なものか多いため、という人には難し過ぎる 入口には一般書も少し置いてあるが、これは近くにビジネスマンが多いからとのことだ すぐ近くに歌舞伎座がある *10AM～7PM.* 休日曜祭日. 中・銀座3-9-2. 543-3604.

Toshiro Mifune, who represents the Japanese samurai warrior to the world, has appeared in 126 films.

Tokyo's **principal commercial district** is called *Ginza* (gin-silver, za-place) after the Tokugawa Shogunate's silver mint which operated in the area from 1612 to 1800.

There are about **760 ambulance calls** per day in Tokyo.

114 Ginza Flag Shop. An unusual shop that has been selling nothing but flags for the past 4 generations. Aside from the *Rising Sun* Japanese flag, US, British, French and other national flags are on sale. The original proprietor was a seaman who raised the Rising Sun at every port. His wife began sewing flags so he would always have an ample supply—when he retired from the sea, it became a business! *Open M-F 10am-6pm. Closed Sa, Su and holidays. 1-20-17 Ginza, Chuo-ku. 561-6053.*

115 Tohgeki Theater. (600 seats) *4-1-1 Tsukiji, Chuo-ku. 541-2711.*

116 Ginza Marunouchi Hotel. *Moderate.* Only a 10-minute walk from the Ginza, this hotel is quiet and pleasant. It has a coffee shop, restaurant, and the **Coronet Bar.** 114 rooms. *4-1-12 Tsukiji, Chuo-ku. 543-5431.*

In 1983, **498 movies were released in Japan.** The number of ticket buyers—174 million in 1983—was one-sixth less than 25 years ago.

114 銀座旗店 めずらしい旗専門の店である 旗しか売っていない店というのも珍しい 現在の女主人で4代目 日の丸のほか、アメリカ、イギリス、フランスなど外国旗も売っている 先代のおじいちゃんが船乗りで、停泊地に着くたびに日の丸を掲げていたそうだ そこでおばあちゃんがせっせと旗作りをしたのがこの店の始まりとか 家庭用の日章旗は木綿製が¥700、絹¥1,000ほど *10AM-6PM.* 休土曜日曜祭日. 中・銀座1-20-17. 561-6053.

115 東劇 （600席）中・築地4-1-1. 541-2711.

116 銀座丸ノ内ホテル 銀座4丁目から歩いて10分のところにある小規模ホテル 比較的静かな場所にあるので落ち着ける 全114室. 狭いロビーの替わりにコーヒーショップを利用するとよい 他にレストラン・バー、コルネットがある. 中・築地4-1-12. 543-5431.

The origin of **Kabuki** as theatrical entertainment is credited to a traveling company of female actresses in the 17th century. Led by **Okuni,** an attendant at a Shinto shrine, the women would stage short comedies and dances on a dry riverbed in Kyoto. Okuni and her actresses quickly became famous, identified as *kabuki*—shocking and out of the ordinary. Kabuki's main reason for popularity was its sensual mode of expression in the dances. Unfortunately, the actresses also practiced prostitution, which prompted the *Tokugawa Shogunate* to prohibit any females to participate in kabuki plays. After a series of tryouts with teenage male actors (resulting in the same dilemma), the Tokugawas instituted several new kabuki policies. *Kyogen,* comical sketches used prior to *Noh* performances, were introduced as necessary elements in the plays. The actors, now males of legal age, were required to use hairpieces, rather than their own hair, to portray women. The players were also ranked, aspiring to become *zagashira* (troupe leader) or *tachioyama* (leading actor for female roles). The Meiji Restoration finally brought new recognition to actors, previously identified with the prostituted *kawaramono* (dry riverbed) people. In our time, a few distinguished kabuki performers are recipients of *The Living Treasure* honor, one of the most prestigious designations for artists in the country.

Close to 10 percent of all earthquakes in the world occur in Japan. The country's earliest tremor, recorded on 23 August in AD 416, was the *Kawachi Earthquake.* Honshu, the main island of Japan, is hit by 2 types of earthquakes: the oceanic, a destructive tremor caused by a Pacific plate wedging far into the earth's crust under the land; and another, much smaller type which does relatively little damage to an isolated area. The largest earthquake ever recorded in Tokyo was the 1923 *Great Kanto,* which measured 7.8 on the Richter scale. Hitting near Tokyo's metro area and Yokohama, it took the lives of more than 100,000 people and caused massive, multi-billion-yen property damage. Over 60,000 people died in Tokyo's central areas, either directly or from the fires that broke out after the quake.

ROME ACCESS

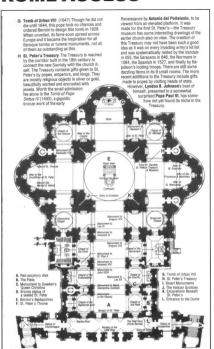

G **Tomb of Urban VIII** (1647) Though he did not die until 1644, this pope took no chances and ordered Bernini to design this tomb in 1628. When unveiled, its fame soon spread across Europe and it became the inspiration for all Baroque tombs or funeral monuments, not all of them as outstanding as this.

H **St. Peter's Treasury** The Treasury is reached by the corridor built in the 18th century to connect the new Sacristy with the church itself. The Treasury contains gifts given to St. Peter's by popes, emperors, and kings. They are mostly religious objects in silver or gold, beautifully worked and encrusted with jewels. Worth the small admission fee alone is the *Tomb of Pope Sixtus IV* (1493), a gigantic bronze work of the early Renaissance by **Antonio del Pollaiuolo**, to be viewed from an elevated platform. It was made for the first St. Peter's—the Treasury museum has some interesting drawings of the earlier church also on view. The creation of this Treasury may not have been such a good idea as it was on every invading army's hit list and was systematically raided by the Vandals in 455, the Saracens in 846, the Normans in 1084, the Spanish in 1527, and finally by Napoleon's looting troops. There are still some dazzling items in its 9 small rooms. The more recent additions to the Treasury include gifts made to popes by visiting heads of state. However, **Lyndon B. Johnson**'s bust of himself, presented to a somewhat surprised **Pope Paul VI**, has somehow not yet found its niche in the Treasury.

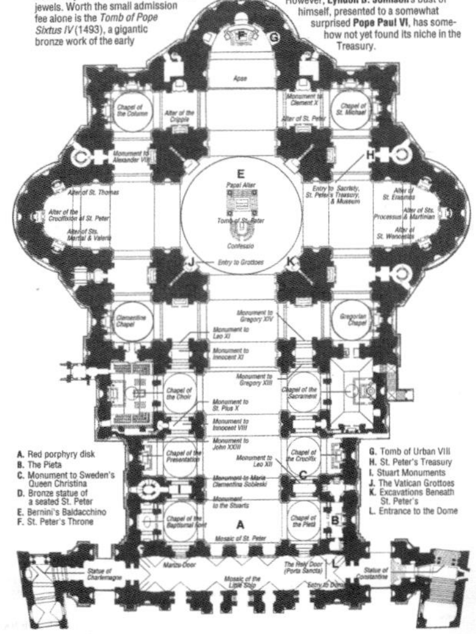

Apse
Chapel of the Column
Altar of the Cripple
Monument to Clement X
Altar of St. Peter
Chapel of St. Michael
Monument to Alexander VII
E
Monument to Leo XI
Monument to Innocent XI
Monument to Gregory XIII
Chapel of the Choir
Chapel of the Sacrament
Monument to St. Pius X
Monument to Innocent VIII
Monument to John XXIII
Chapel of the Presentation
Monument to Leo XII
Chapel of the Crucifix
Monument to Maria Clementina Sobieski
Monument to the Stuarts
Chapel of the Baptismal Font
Chapel of the Pietà
Mosaic of St. Peter
Statue of Charlemagne
The Holy Door (Porta Sancta)
Mosaic of the Little Ship
Statue of Constantine
A. Red porphyry disk
B. The Pieta
C. Monument to Sweden's Queen Christina
D. Bronze statue of a seated St. Peter
E. Bernini's Baldacchino
F. St. Peter's Throne
G. Tomb of Urban VIII
H. St. Peter's Treasury
I. Stuart Monuments
J. The Vatican Grottoes
K. Excavations Beneath St. Peter's
L. Entrance to the Dome

I **Stuart Monuments** In 1820 **Antonio Canova**, one-time honorary president of Philadelphia's Academy of Fine Arts, designed this highly original monument to the last of the Stuarts: **James III** (who died in 1766) and his sons, **Bonnie Prince Charlie** and **Cardinal Henry Stuart**, the Duke of York. The Stuarts settled in Rome after fleeing England with the English Royal Seal. When Cardinal Henry Stuart returned it to **King George IV** in the 1820s, the British monarch graciously paid for the actual Stuart tomb, in the Vatican grottoes. Facing it is the monument to James' wife, **Mary Clementine Sobieski**, where the inscription is written—and history rewritten—*Queen of England, France and Ireland* (obvious confusion with her predecessor Mary Queen of Scots).

J **The Vatican Grottoes** This crypt lies between St. Peter's present floor and the mostly demolished ruins of the first church built by **Constantine**. Some pillars of the older church are visible in the grottoes, which contain the tombs of many popes, including the only English pope, **Nicholas Breakspear**, who in 1154 took the name of **Hadrian IV**. **Popes Pius II, Pius XII, John XXIII, Paul VI**, and **John Paul I** have their tombs here as well. The entry to the grottoes is reached by a narrow staircase behind either the giant statues by Bernini of **St. Andrew** or that opposite of **St. Longinus**, the latter being a Roman centurion who pierced Christ's side with his lance and who was later converted. The obligatory exit is near the **Holy Year Door** in the church's portico.

K **Excavations Beneath St. Peter's** (gli Scavi) In 1939, when workers were preparing a tomb for **Pius XI** in the grottoes, they accidently came upon parts of the first St. Peter's church and beneath that a pagan and a Christian graveyard. The pagan tombs date from the 2nd and 3rd centuries AD and are more numerous and brightly decorated. It is a miniature necropolis. The Christian tombs are more impoverished and date from the 2nd century. One niche, containing human and animal bones, has scratched on it a grafitto that has convinced one Vatican cryptographer that it says *Peter is here*. One problem is that St. Peter's skull has been venerated for at least 1000 years in Rome's cathedral of St. John Lateran and this niche contained most of a human cranium.

The legend that Peter was crucified and quickly buried by his followers just outside the walls of Nero's Circus is, however, very strong. The excavations are not open to the general public, but anyone with some qualifications can write well in advance for permission to go on one of the small, infrequent guided tours. The expert serving as guide may not always speak English. The visit takes about one hour.

To join a tour of these ruins, write ahead to the Office of Excavations, Vatican City, giving several possible dates. No children under 14 admitted. If it is low season, a telephone call (6985314) might produce the good news that one of the tours has an opening the next day.

L. **Entrance to the Dome** Take the elevator or stairs to the inside of the dome, where your first thrill may be looking down on the people 160 feet below, encircling the papal altar and looking smaller than the Barberini bees had just looked. From there, another staircase goes up to a gallery 238 feet above the

church's floor. If this is not enough, there are more stairs, still within the shell of the dome, taking you 322 feet above ground level. The intrepid climber can then take a narrow spiral staircase to the exterior gallery (where you'll be 352 feet above the altar that runs around the lantern of the world's highest brick dome). If you do not make the entire climb, you can wait for your companions on the wind-swept rooftop, where there is a coffee bar and a miniature Vatican post office.

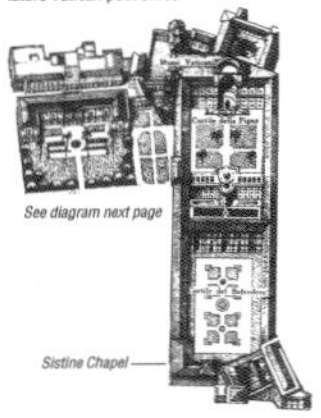

Musei Vaticani
Cortile della Pigna
See diagram next page
Sistine Chapel

20 **Vatican Museums (Musei Vaticani)** The single entrance for all the museums is on Viale del Vaticano, a brisk 15-minute walk from St. Peter's Square down the Via di Porta Angelica (also the terminus of the 64 bus line). Though there is no risk of losing one's way since you just follow the walls, it can become unpleasant if you collide with groups of tourists going the other way on the narrow stretch of the sidewalk. A bus that departs from (and returns to) a spot near the orange sign in St. Peter's Square, and also takes you across the Vatican gardens en route, may be a better bet if there are not too many people waiting for it. Do visit the museums in the early hours because they are far less crowded, and the ticket window shuts at 1PM in winter and 4PM during the peak tourist season. St. Peter's is one of the few churches in Rome that does not shut at noon for the lunch break and is open until 6PM in winter and 7PM in summer, so it makes sense to go there after you have seen the museums. As soon as you find the muse-

Piazza del Popolo

(Reshaped 1816-1820, **Giuseppe Valadier**) This square was the first part of Rome that pilgrims saw as they arrived from the north through **Porta del Popolo**. When **Queen Christina of Sweden** renounced her throne to become a Catholic and live in Rome, **Pope Alexander VII** had **Bernini** remodel the inner face of the porta for her arrival in 1655.

1 **Obelisk** The largest obelisk in Rome was brought here in 1589 from **Circus Maximus**. It was brought from Egypt by the first emperor of Rome, **Augustus**, around 10 BC and is over 3000 years old.

2 **Santa Maria del Popolo** (1099, architect unknown) This church is tucked into the Walls of Rome and built over the supposed tomb of **Nero** to chase away his ghost, which haunted the area. His wife was buried in a pyramid across the square, where **Rosati's** bar now stands. In 1477, during the reign of **Pope Sixtus IV**, this church was rebuilt. It contains a treasure chest of fabulous paintings from **Raphael** to **Pinturicchio**, from **Sansovino** to **Caravaggio**. The remains of **Cattanei Vanozza** and her murdered son, the **Duke of Gandia**, lie here. She was the mistress of **Alexander VI**, the Borgia pope; their other 2 children were **Cesare** and the beautiful **Lucrezia**. Cesare's ambition knew no bounds; he forced his attentions on his sister, murdered his brother, and finally perished because of it. The great *bon vivant* and brilliant patron of the arts, **Agostino Chigi**, is also buried here.

Porta del Popolo
Pincio
Piazza del Popolo

3 **Rosati** Enjoy the symmetry of Piazza del Popolo at what many say is the best café in Rome. The Rosati family has been serving visitors and Romans alike for 3 generations. They say there's a restaurant upstairs, but we've never heard of anyone going there. ♦ M, W-Su 7:30AM-midnight. Piazza del Popolo 5A. 3225859, 3611418

4 **Canova** The rival to Rosati's bar. Where the sun-lovers go to sit n' soak, in good weather. Named after the early 19th-century Venetian sculptor **Antonio Canova**, famed for his full frontal of Napoleon's sister Pauline (see **Villa Borghese** on page 29). Recently renovated. ♦ Piazza del Popolo 16. 3612231, 3612227

5 **Santa Maria dei Miracoli and Santa Maria di Monte Santo** (1679, C. **Rainaldi** with help from **Bernini** and **Fontana**) The design of these churches was based on the idea that as pilgrims entered Rome, these 2 seemingly identical buildings would welcome them with an example of the majestic quality of Rome. Rainaldi struggled and magnificently triumphed in making them appear the same, although the plots of land on which they stand are quite different—one church is round, the other elliptical.

6 **Dal Bolognese** ★★$$$ A chic restaurant where you can go and hope to be noticed, but failing that, you can look around and hope to see somebody worth noticing. Some critics claim that the fashion outshines the cooking, but the trolley of boiled meats with a delectable green sauce has earned its fame. Also good are figs (when in season) and prosciutto, pasta, and *carpaccio* (paper-thin raw beef with Parmesan and *rughetta*). To finish off the meal, try the gooey trifle. ♦ Closed Monday, Sunday night, and part of August. Piazza del Popolo 1. Reservations required. 3611426

7 **Studio S** Carmine Siniscalco presides over Rome's top gallery, where a vernissage is

both a social and an artistic event. ♦ Via della Penna 59. 3612086

8 **Hotel Locarno** $$ One of the most attractive of the intimate neighborhood hotels in downtown Rome. No restaurant, but a cozy bar. Here the décor is Art Nouveau. Thirty-eight rooms, one suite. ♦ Via della Penna 22. 3610841, 3610060; fax 3604898

9 **Osteria St. Ana** ★★$$ Rather "in" place with suave Italians and the international movie crowd. Rough, white-washed country walls and a plethora of pictures on the wall make this cozy celler feel like an art gallery. Know that the antipasto laid out on your table is not a gift—taste it and it will show up on your bill! This is not one of the restaurants that include a glass of bubbly or a bite of pâté in the cover charge. (Roman cover charges vary from one to 6000 lire and often are not marked on the menu as they should be.) Perhaps the best filet mignon in Rome. ♦ Via della Penna 68. 3610291

10 **59** ★★$$$ Many people swear by this restaurant and rave about the food, but we find the ambiance cold and the service precious. The specialties are from Bologna, one of the meccas of Italian cuisine. The inspiration came from Rome's contemporary restaurateuse, **Ceasarina**, who has unfortunately gone on to the land of the great *grillade. Ave!* ♦ Closed Saturday (June-July), Sunday, and August. Via A. Brunetti 59. Reservations recommended. 3619019

Restaurants/Clubs: Red
Hotels: Blue
Shops/Parks: Green
Sights/Culture: Black

Along the Tiber

The ancient Romans honored the river gods, and small wonder. For better and sometimes for worse, the Tiber River has always dominated Rome's life. The river provided the ports for merchandise, from marble to wine, that was imported from the far corners of the Empire, and the city's first marketplace was at the river's edge. The **Forum Boarium** (bovine market), a trading post where animals and hides could be swapped or a goatskin of wine bartered for a clay pot, was probably established in the eighth century BC. On the down side, the Tiber flooded the **Pantheon** and the **Roman Forum**, and its high-water markers can be spotted on the walls of many a building in the oldest quarters of the city.

For the first 16 centuries of Rome's existence, anyone who could avoided living in the marshy and malaria-ridden areas bordering the river. This worked to Hadrian's advantage as it gave him open space to build his mausoleum here in AD 139. Through the centuries, this monument (now the **Castel Sant'Angelo**) slowly became transformed into a fortress. It eventually became so strong that in 1377, when the papacy returned to Rome from exile in Avignon, the pontiff and his court claimed it as their personal citadel—it was connected to the **Vatican** by an enclosed passageway—and site of the papal prisons. For centuries, the adjacent bridge, **Ponte Sant'Angelo,** bore the heavy traffic of religious pilgrims making their way to **St. Peter's Basilica.** During the Renaissance, **Via Giulia,** connecting to the **Vatican Bridge** (now called **Ponte Vittorio Emanuele**), was designed to provide an alternative route. The street soon became one of the most popular addresses for the newly wealthy and many a palazzo was built along it, with backyards facing the Tiber. Today the mile-long street is a pedestrians-only shopping area, lined with antiques shops and charming restaurants.

The **Aurelian Walls,** which gave protection to Trastevere for the first time, were built in AD 271. When that area became popular, the Jews who lived there were displaced to other side of the Tiber, to a district that became a locked **Ghetto** in the 16th century. Today about 2,000 Jews still live in this neighborhood, and it is considered prime real estate, with a bustling business community and good bargain shopping. Just south of it are the ruins of the **Circus Maximus,** the stadium where the chariot races of ancient times took place.

Floating between the Ghetto and Trastevere, **Isola Tiberina** (Tiber Island) has served as a hospital site for over 2,000 years. Ancient Romans took their sickly slaves there to die; later, plague victims were abandoned to their fate; still later, monks built teaching hospitals here.

Until the late 19th century most of the Tiber was lined with mills for grinding wheat, their wheels turned by the action of the river as it flowed toward Ostia and the sea. Swarms of seagulls now reside in the Tiber, and in winter cormorants from North Europe join them. Today's visitors photograph the birds, the fishers in their boats, the recreational scullers at their oars, and the great church domes reflected in the waters.

Castel Sant'Angelo

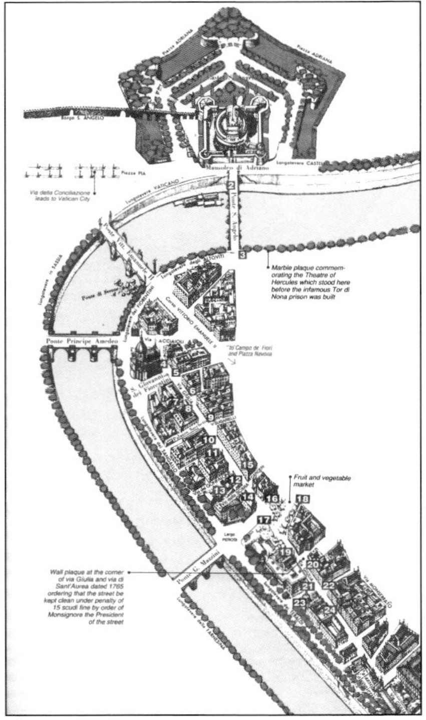

Mausoleo di Adriano
Via della Conciliazione leads to Vatican City
Marble plaque commemorating the Theatre of Hercules which stood here before the infamous Tor di Nona prison was built
Ponte Principe Amedeo
Fruit and vegetable market
Wall plaque at the corner of via Giulia and via di Sant'Aurea dated 1765 ordering that the street be kept clean under penalty of 15 scudi fine by order of Monsignore the President of the street

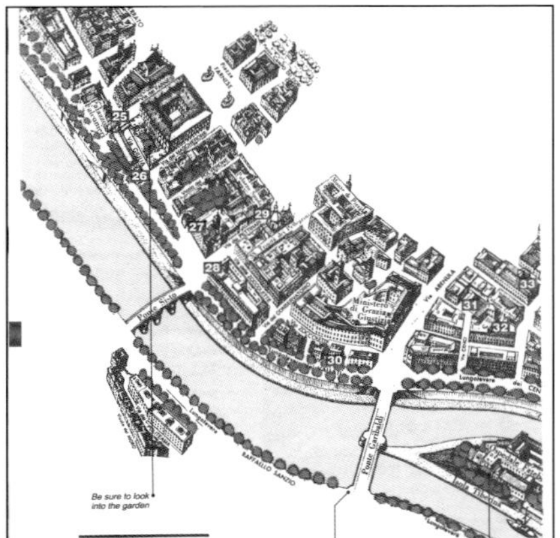

Be sure to look into the garden
Ponte Garibaldi
Associazione Amici del Tevere (Friends of the Tiber) sponsors boat trips that leave from just below Ponte Garibaldi on the Trastevere side
Tiber Island

Castel Sant'Angelo

1 **Castel Sant'Angelo** (AD 139, architect **Antonino Pio**) The bulk of this structure (illustrated on page 30) dates from AD 135, when Emperor Hadrian built it as his family mausoleum. Personal grandeur prompted the monument, but so did necessity: There was no space left across the river in the older imperial burial chamber, the **Mausoleum of Augustus.** The building originally looked something like a tiered wedding cake atop a square platter: the foundation, about 275 feet on each side, supported a circular tomb of marble-faced brick; a columned portico 210 feet in circumference and 164 feet high ran around the tomb; and on top of that was a small round temple surrounded by a garden planted with cypresses. Statues adorned the upper parapets, including one of Hadrian as a sun god driving a four-horse chariot.

With the building of the **Aurelian Walls** around the city in the third century, the mausoleum became located inside the Roman defenses; this was the beginning of its transformation from monument to fortress. When Goths attacked the city in 410, Romans fled into the tomb for refuge; they even hurled some of Hadrian's statues down on the enemies below. (Luckily some survived: *The Dancing Faun* is now in Florence's Uffizi Gallery and *The Sleeping Faun* resides in Munich.)

The building acquired its present name in the year 590. The city was suffering an outbreak of plague, so Pope Gregory the Great ordered all Romans to participate in a procession to the **Vatican** to pray for an end to the crisis. Hundreds died while on the march, but Gregory saw a vision of the Archangel Michael hovering over Hadrian's tomb, sheathing his sword—an obvious answer to their prayers. A statue of St. Michael was soon hoisted atop

the mausoleum, a chapel built inside, and the name officially changed to **Castel Sant'Angelo.**

About 900 years later, in the medieval power struggle between the papacy and the noble Roman families, the castle's conversion to fortress was completed. The square base was chipped away to create a protective hollow ring inside it; stout walls and four corner towers were added. The popes moved from their traditional **Lateran Palace** residence into the **Vatican** and constructed a half-mile-long fortified passageway connecting it to the safety of **Castel Sant'Angelo.** But life inside the fortress walls was not altogether barren. In 1492 Alexander VI, the Borgia pope, built a sumptuous apartment with all the requisite creature comforts and handsome frescoed walls (some of which were restored in 1994). Of course, it was pretty grim for those who were not in the fortress by choice: This was also the papal prison and the site of capital punishments.

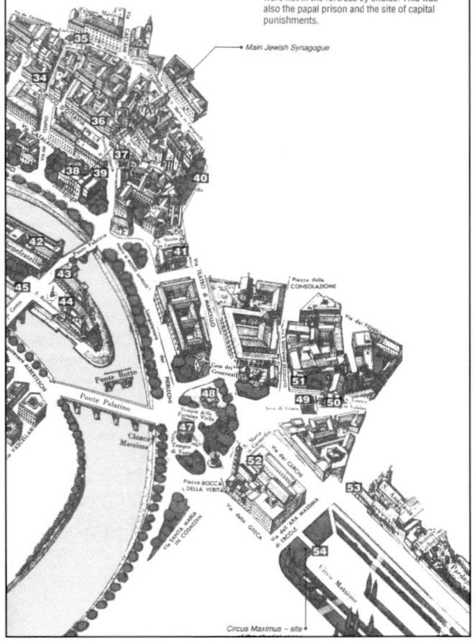

Main Jewish Synagogue
Circus Maximus – site

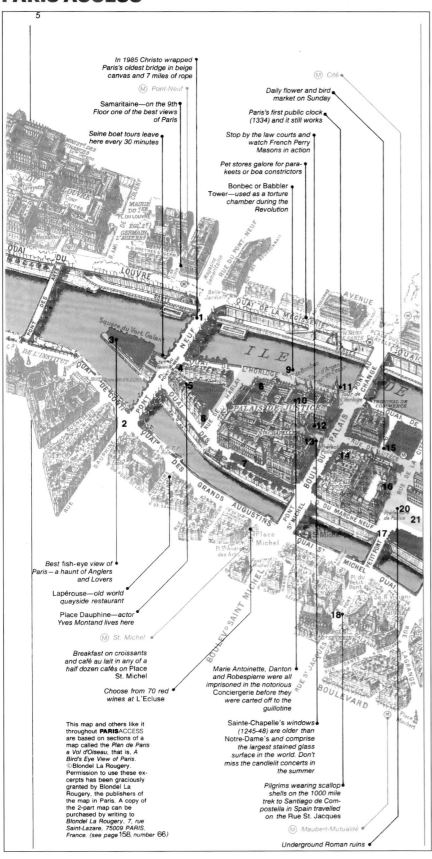

In 1985 Christo wrapped Paris's oldest bridge in beige canvas and 7 miles of rope

Ⓜ *Pont-Neuf*

Samaritaine—on the 9th Floor one of the best views of Paris

Seine boat tours leave here every 30 minutes

Ⓜ *Cité*

Daily flower and bird market on Sunday

Paris's first public clock (1334) and it still works

Stop by the law courts and watch French Perry Masons in action

Pet stores galore for parakeets or boa constrictors

Bonbec or Babbler Tower—used as a torture chamber during the Revolution

Best fish-eye view of Paris—a haunt of Anglers and Lovers

Lapérouse—old world quayside restaurant

Place Dauphine—actor Yves Montand lives here

Ⓜ *St. Michel*

Breakfast on croissants and café au lait in any of a half dozen cafés on Place St. Michel

Choose from 70 red wines at L'Ecluse

Marie Antoinette, Danton and Robespierre were all imprisoned in the notorious Conciergerie before they were carted off to the guillotine

Sainte-Chapelle's windows (1245-48) are older than Notre-Dame's and comprise the largest stained glass surface in the world. Don't miss the candlelit concerts in the summer

Pilgrims wearing scallop shells on the 1000 mile trek to Santiago de Compostela in Spain travelled on the Rue St. Jacques

Ⓜ *Maubert-Mutualité*

Underground Roman ruins

This map and others like it throughout **PARIS**ACCESS are based on sections of a map called the *Plan de Paris a Vol d'Oiseau*, that is, *A Bird's Eye View of Paris*. ©Blondel La Rougery. Permission to use these excerpts has been graciously granted by Blondel La Rougery, the publishers of the map in Paris. A copy of the 2-part map can be purchased by writing to Blondel La Rougery, 7, rue Saint-Lazare, 75009 PARIS, France. (see page 158, number 66.)

6

The Islands: Ile de la Cité / Ile St. Louis

At the heart of Paris are two islands: **Ile de la Cité**, sloop-shaped and cradling **Notre-Dame** in its stern, towing **Ile St. Louis** in its wake. Although the islands have no grand hotels, banks, major restaurants, theaters, or designer shops, they do possess two gems of Gothic architecture (Notre-Dame and **Sainte-Chapelle**), a world-famous prison, an elegant 17th century subdivision, some of Paris's most beautiful private mansions, the nation's law courts and police headquarters, an Art Nouveau metro station, a flower and bird market, 15 bridges, and one too many souvenir shops selling miniature Napoleon busts and *I love Paris* bumper stickers.

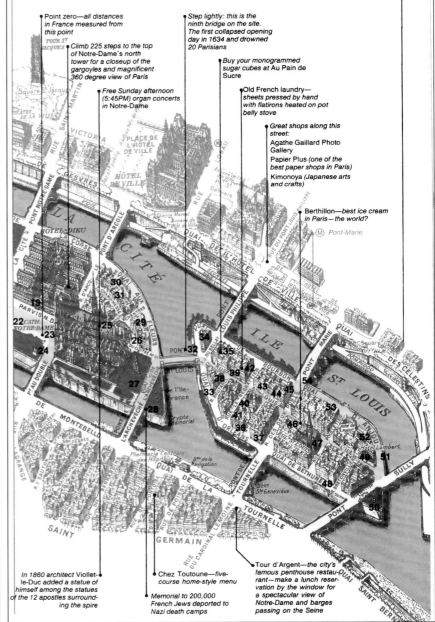

Point zero—all distances in France measured from this point

Climb 225 steps to the top of Notre-Dame's north tower for a closeup of the gargoyles and magnificent 360 degree view of Paris

Free Sunday afternoon (5:45PM) organ concerts in Notre-Dame

Step lightly: this is the ninth bridge on the site. The first collapsed opening day in 1634 and drowned 20 Parisians

Buy your monogrammed sugar cubes at Au Pain de Sucre

Old French laundry— sheets pressed by hand with flatirons heated on pot belly stove

Great shops along this street:
Agathe Gaillard Photo Gallery
Papier Plus (one of the best paper shops in Paris)
Kimonoya (Japanese arts and crafts)

Berthillon—best ice cream in Paris—the world?

Ⓜ *Pont-Marie*

In 1860 architect Viollet-le-Duc added a statue of himself among the statues of the 12 apostles surrounding the spire

Chez Toutoune—five-course home-style menu

Memorial to 200,000 French Jews deported to Nazi death camps

Tour d'Argent—the city's famous penthouse restaurant—make a lunch reservation by the window for a spectacular view of Notre-Dame and barges passing on the Seine

USAtlas
1990s

“

A map is a pattern made understandable.

”

The epiphany I had when I looked at the Rand McNally atlas was that you don't drive across the United States alphabetically. That's sort of a joke, but it's the truth; you don't drive alphabetically, you drive state to state and my atlas was organized state by state, and there was a key map showing where you were in the US going from one state to the other. It came about when I moved to New York from LA, living and working in a loft space in Soho and realized to survive in New York, if you wanted to be a player, it was sensible to get a little house out in the Hamptons. Well, I didn't have that much money so I got a terminally cute little Victorian house on the wrong side of the highway.

Then I had to buy a car, and I had to know how to get around but I was living in a city I hadn't lived in before and going to Long Island which I hadn't been to before. So I got the Rand McNally atlas, then one of the top-selling books in soft cover, which is tough to imagine because they're so ungainly. Every state in there took up a page. All road atlases were developed from information that came from each state and since every state's a different size, every map is a different scale. At each state line, there was a huge change, like a science fiction movie, all of a sudden you had one scale and then were in another, the maps filled with little numbers and arrows from here to there and the highway numbers and everything else. They were ungainly to use in the car, and were spiral bound and the pages were always coming out of the spiral. It was a terrible product that was very popular at the time; Rand McNally was one of the most well-known companies. But everything disappears: of the 500 biggest companies in America in 1900, only 16 are left. The fact that the Rand McNally road atlas is not a primo product any more is understandable, but at a time when things are popular, you realize they won't be forever. Twitter, Facebook and other products we have now won't be here in 100 years, there will be something else, everything is going to change. So I wanted my own atlas with all maps to the same scale where the fundamental way to find where to go is on the cover, you didn't have to page through the book alphabetically, every map related to the human experience. You can drive about 250 miles a day comfortably. You stop for lunch, you stop to pee, you stop to get gas, and it's about five hours of driving. You can drive more, but that's an understandable unit. So I divided the 250 miles into 50-mile grids and 50 miles was about an hour. You don't need miles; they don't mean anything because when you're driving you care about time, not miles. The map was 5 hours by 5 hours, 250 miles by 250 miles. If you were in one of those 250-mile grids and saw another square that was a city, 25 miles becomes important: The centroid of 25 miles is 12.5 miles, and a 12.5-mile ring around the city is when you make a decision to drive through it or around it. And sometimes in that 25-mile square you can have another one of 5 miles, about as big as the heart of any city, showing street names, hotels and major places. Those are dumb, human things. I don't think you could make dumber decisions. It cost a fortune to do the book, it used all new maps.

At that time, the NeXT computer was put out by Steve Jobs who called me and wanted to incorporate the atlas into the computer. We were going to meet in San Francisco where I had a 70-person office because I was doing the Yellow Pages directory for Pac Bell, but then he sold the software for a huge amount of money and came back on board with Apple. The atlas was a good book; we made modifications of various Abode programs to do it and it was the most intense system using Adobe for mapping. They told us it was a model for what they could do and later incorporated it into other programs. It was a breakthrough book and I thought it'd be my annuity, but it wasn't, it was fiscally impossible. I sold several hundred thousands to a rental car company, and it was received very well; you could fold it in half and put it in the glove compartment. It is still an excellent book, but there's no reason for it if you have a screen in your car or your smart phone. But it was a very good book and I'm proud of it. **RSW**

EVACUTAION GRID

Dwight D. Eisenhower initiated the construction of the interstate highway system partly in his belief of the inevitability of WW3. Evacuating parts of the United States and the landing of aircraft had high priority.

The evacuation plan was to have 2 systems of roads (north-south and east-west, shown below). Airstrips occured with the design of the road system which specified a straightaway every certain number of miles. He also had a shadow cabinet that met monthly and only informed JFK at his ignauguration.

Major U.S. Interstates, North-South

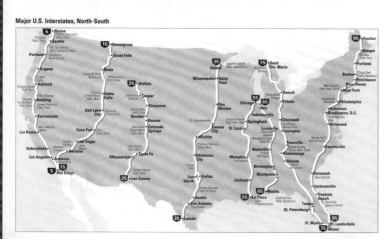

Beginning to End	Length	Driving Time (no stops)	Don't Miss
5 Blaine, Washington to San Diego, California	1,382 miles	29 hours, 55 min.	Disneyland
15 Sweetgrass, Montana to San Diego, California	1,437 miles	31 hours, 45 min.	Zion Natl. Park
25 Buffalo, Wyoming to Las Cruces, New Mexico	1,062 miles	23 hours, 25 min.	Florissant Fossil Beds
35 Duluth, Minnesota to Laredo, Texas	1,568 miles	33 hours, 40 min.	The Alamo
55 Chicago, Illinois to La Place, Louisiana	944 miles	21 hours, 40 min.	Graceland
65 Gary, Indiana to Mobile, Alabama	888 miles	19 hours, 45 min.	Grand Ole Opry
75 Sault Ste. Marie, Michigan to Miami, Florida	1,787 miles	39 hours, 50 min.	Kentucky Horse Park
95 Houlton, Maine to Miami, Florida	1,894 miles	41 hours, 5 min.	Sea Islands

Major U.S. Interstates, West-East

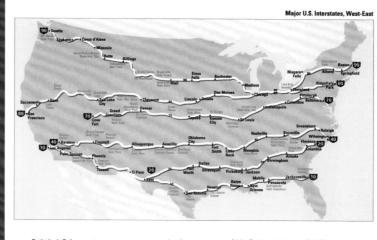

Beginning to End	Length	Driving Time (no stops)	Don't Miss
90 Seattle, Washington to Boston, Massachusetts	3,163 miles	53 hours, 47 min.	Yellowstone
80 San Francisco, California to Ridgefield Park, New Jersey	2,907 miles	51 hours, 35 min.	Great Salt Lake
70 Cove Fort, Utah to Baltimore, Maryland	2,175 miles	36 hours, 34 min.	Mt. Evans Highway
40 Barstow, California to Wilmington, North Carolina	2,463 miles	45 hours, 20 min.	Great Smokies
20 Kent, Texas to Florence, South Carolina	1,536 miles	26 hours, 39 min.	Vicksburg Natl. Park
10 Los Angeles, California to Jacksonville, Florida	2,460 miles	41 hours, 34 min.	Okefenokee Swamp

61

2
Table of Contents

Key to the Maps

→ Park or State Rec. Area with camping
• Cities with a population over 5,000
• Points of Interest
→ Mountain Pass
• An enlarged map appears on page 110
— Tertiary roads
— Non-accessible road connections
— Tunnel
• Cities with a population over 100,000
— Freeways (Controlled access roads)
• Cities with a population less than 5,000
— Secondary roads
— Toll highway

3
Table of Contents

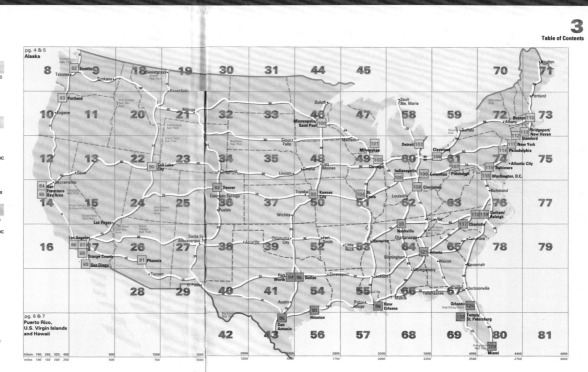

The United States, organized the way you drive it. Each page represents 250x250 miles, with all 48 mainland states mapped at the same scale. Interesting local notes apear on every page.

The most Americans ever involved in a battle on US soil met on 1-3 July 1863 at Gettysburg, PA (A3). 51,000 were killed or wounded. Lincoln's Address, by the way, was written on neither the back nor the front of an envelope. He wrote 2 full-length drafts.

5 million visitors come to stare, visit, buy and otherwise invade Pennsylvania Dutch Country—west of Philadelphia, PA. Don't visit on Sunday—everything's closed. Tourist Information: 717/299-8901

You know this is the largest suburb of New York, but did you know that the Census Bureau says New Jersey is the only state in which 100% of the population lives in a metropolitan area?

The summer popularity of the Jersey and Delaware Shores is well justified, but if you can get here in late September the weather is usually still pleasant and the crowds—thankfully—have gone home.

"O say can you see"—it would've been hard to miss the flag praised at Fort McHenry (B4)—it was the largest battle flag ever flown, 30' x 42'. Who wrote our national anthem? See page 156.

New Jersey Tourist Information: 609/292-2470

Delaware Tourist Information: 1-800-441-8846

Maryland Tourist Information: 301/333-6611

New Jersey Road Information: 201/344-1704

Delaware Road Information: 302/736-5851

Maryland Road Information: 301/486-3101

← pg. 61

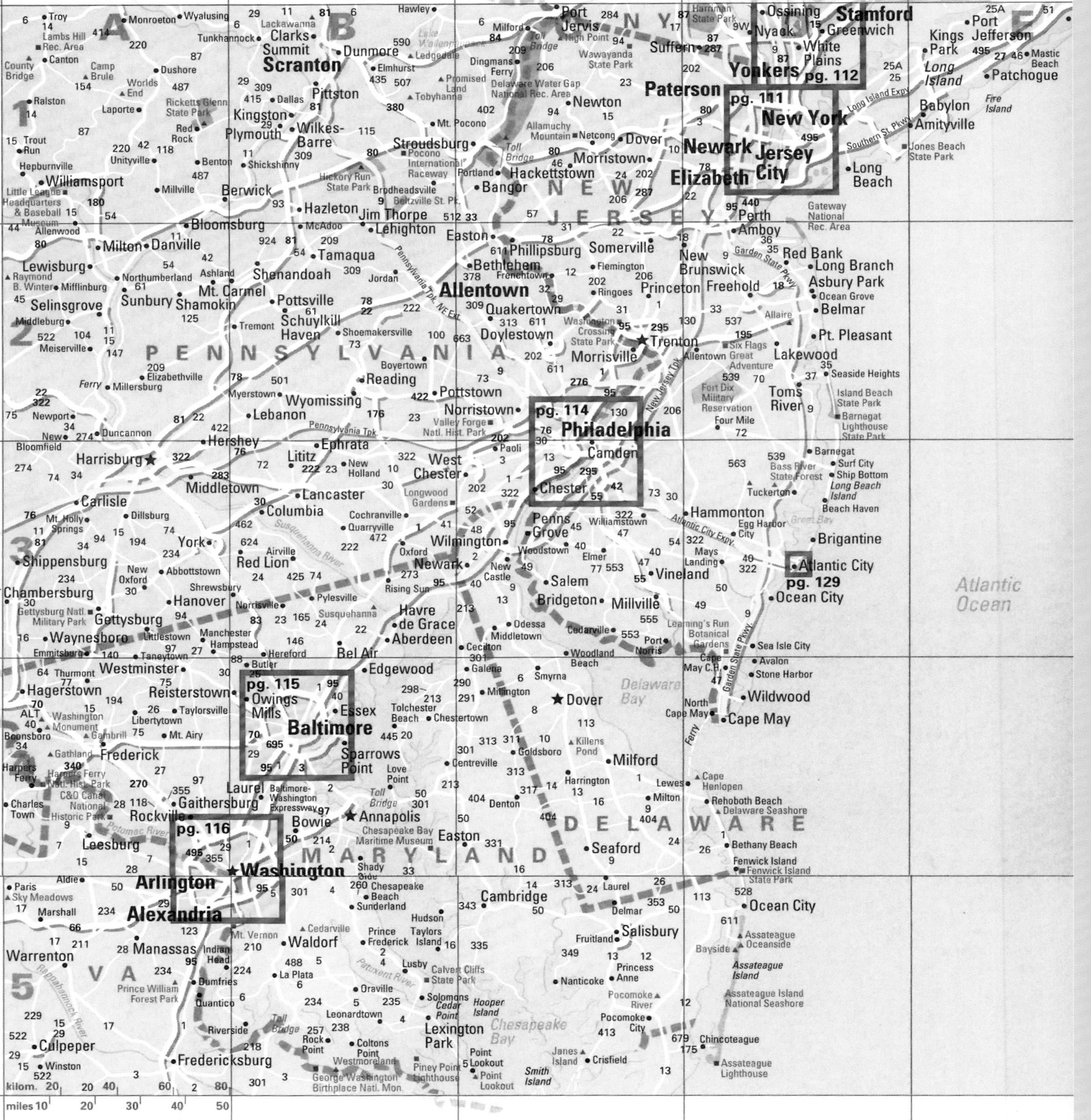

The map on this page is 250x250 miles.

N

25x25 miles

40 major metropolitan centers are marked in yellow on the 250x250 mile detail. We give you a sense of the city - whether you drive into it or around it.

The five boroughs of Manhattan, Brooklyn, Queens, Staten Island and the Bronx united to form New York City in 1898. With a population of three million, the new city instantly qualified as the largest city in the world.

Join the fun. You and nearly 18 million other folks will visit the Big Apple this year.

New York is no place to learn how to drive—in fact, if you're under 18 you're forbidden to drive, by law. You cannot turn right on red here, you know.

The city is just over 300 miles square; the population density is about 26,000 people per square mile. Does that help explain New Yorkers?

A tough town with a heart: nearly 1/5 of the land in New York is devoted to parks and playgrounds. Visit the Brooklyn Botanic Garden (C4) for some beautiful greenery.

There's over three-quarters of a million college students here. Only 10 cities in the US have entire populations as large.

Want a great deal? The Staten Island Ferry costs a *quarter*, with an incomparable view of the world's most famous skyline—and lady Liberty, too.

The Verrazano Narrows Bridge (B5), is the world's longest suspension bridge.

Tourist Information:
212/397-8222

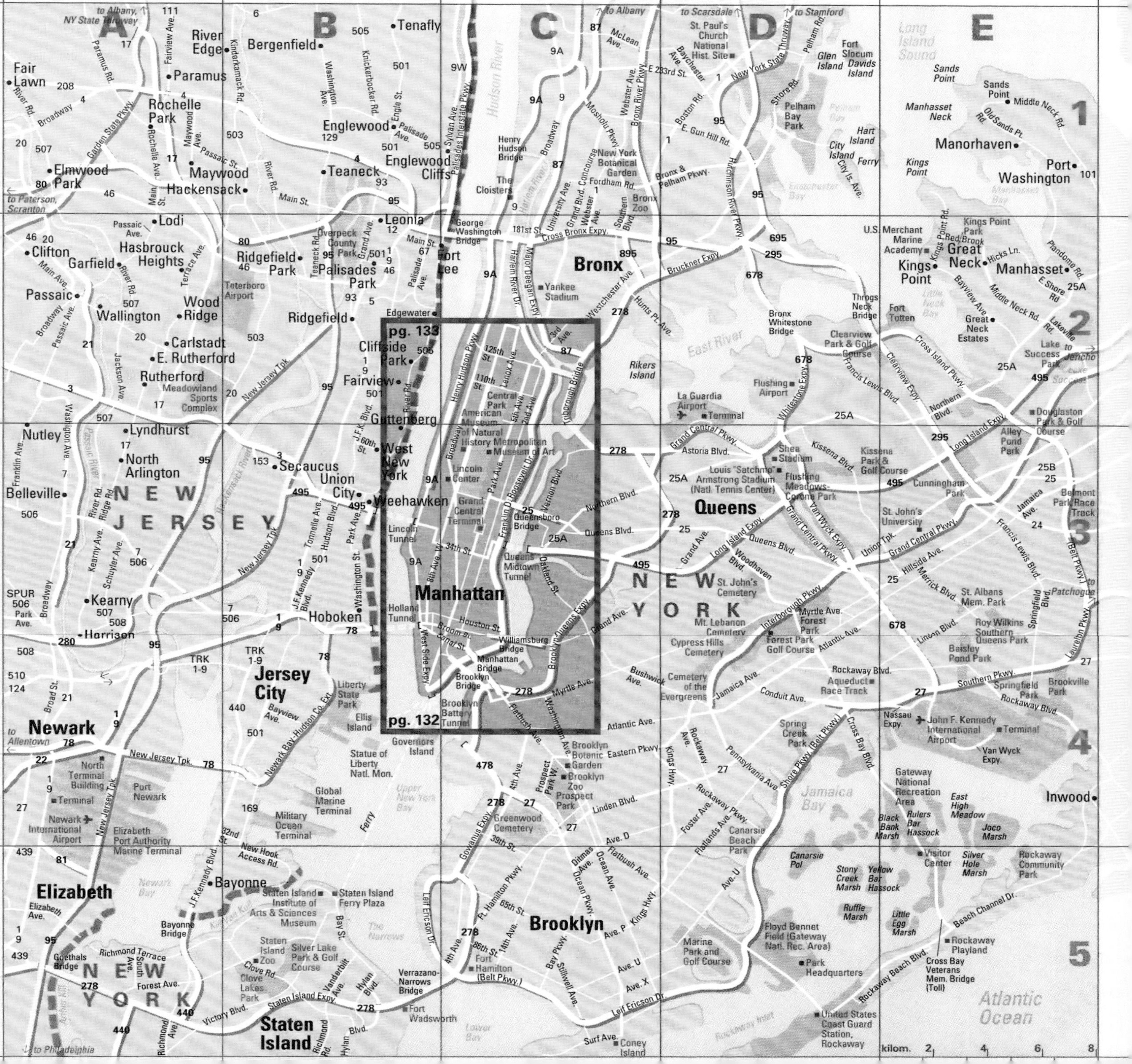

map on this page
25x25 miles.

pg. 133

pg. 132

N

Manhattan

Bronx

Queens

Brooklyn

Staten Island

NEW JERSEY

NEW YORK

Newark

Elizabeth

Jersey City

Hoboken

Atlantic Ocean

Peter Minuit, we all know, bought Manhattan for $24—a good deal that a successor of his blew when the Dutch accepted a colony in South America from the British in trade for the magic isle.

The "Wall" on Wall Street was constructed to keep the Indians out—doesn't do much good against modern-day hostiles.

When kids draw a skyscraper, inevitably the result is the Chrysler Building (E3) ... a beautiful caricature of a tall building.

Another old favorite, the Empire State Building (E2), hosts the Run Up every February. Racers climb all 1,575 steps to the top of the building as fast as possible (about 14 minutes). Whew!

You want great food? Try the Fulton Fish Market (B2)—the catch of the day is you have to be there by 6 a.m.

There's more to shopping here than Saks; you want to shop like a New Yorker, go to Canal Street (C2). Ready, set, haggle!

A real shopping adventure is Chinatown (C2). Shop the produce stands and sample things you've never heard of—like 100-year-old eggs.

Only China has more Chinese. And Athens more Greeks, San Juan more Puerto Ricans, Dublin more Irish and Israel more Jews. Where else could they have put the United Nations (E3)?

Learn all the essentials about this great, confusing, exhilarating city in my New York ACCESS Guide.

Recommended hotels—

Expensive:
The Grand Hyatt
1-800-233-1234
The Helmsley Park Lane
1-800-221-4982
Hotel Parker Meridien
1-800-543-4300
Hotel Pierre
1-800-332-3442
The Mayfair Regent
1-800-223-0542
New York Hilton and Towers
1-800-445-8667
The Plaza
1-800-228-3000
The Regency Hotel
1-800-233-2356
The Waldorf Astoria
1-800-445-8667
The United Nations Plaza Hotel
1-800-233-1234

Moderate:
The Algonquin
1-800-548-0345
The Dorset
1-800-227-2348
The Empire
1-800-545-7400
The Gramercy Park Hotel
1-800-221-4083
The Mayflower Hotel
1-800-223-4164
The Milford Plaza
1-800-528-1234
The Roosevelt
1-800-223-1870
The Royalton
1-800-635-9013
Sheraton Centre
1-800-325-3535
The Warwick Hotel
1-800-223-4099

The map on this page is 5x5 miles.

A　B　C　D　E

1　2　3　4　5

Hudson River

Manhattan

Brooklyn

East River

Don't be afraid of the subway. Sure it's dirty and noisy, but there is no better, faster way between points in this huge place. And are you sure you're up for a New York cab ride? Remember, America's first speeding arrest was here. In 1899 a cabbie was pulled over for careening down Lexington Avenue at 12 miles per hour.

New York Sons of Liberty had their own Tea Party in 1774, boarding the *London* and dumping 18 cases of tea into the East River.

New York is home to lots of spectacular museums, as well as the world's largest. That would be The American Museum of Natural History *(B2)*.

It's probably disputable—but New York does claim the world's first "real" apartment building (1869). There are now so many apartments here, that the Upper East Side's 10021 ZIP code requires the largest residential postal station in the world. One apartment building alone has 850 boxes and requires three mail carriers to make deliveries.

When the Cathedral of St. John the Divine *(D3)* is finished, it will be the largest in the world.

New York City average daily high temperatures:

J	38.0°	J	85.3°
F	40.1°	A	83.7°
M	48.6°	S	76.4°
A	61.1°	O	65.6°
M	71.5°	N	53.6°
J	80.1°	D	42.1°

5x5 miles

11 downtown centers are marked in orange on the 25x25 maps. Each area shows the area covered by a 5x5 mile section of the city.

The map on this page is 5x5 miles.

66

*Where am I and what
is around me?*

99

Newport and Charleston 1990s

THE NEWPORT GUIDE The beach stone on the front cover was carved by John Benson, master stone carver. Front cover photographed by Richard Benson, former Dean of Yale School of Art.

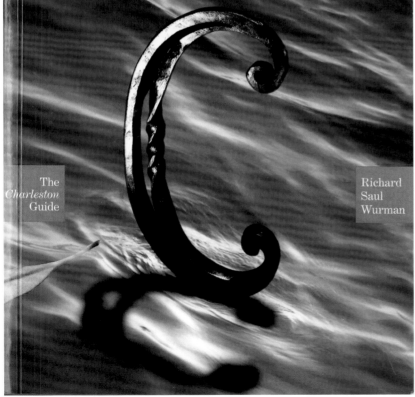

THE CHARLESTON GUIDE The C on the front cover was wrought by Charlestonian Philip Simmons (1912-2009), Master Ironworker and National Heritage Fellow.

I moved to Newport, and it was the same story as moving to LA – I didn't know Newport, there was no good guidebook so I thought I'd do my own. It's a sweet little thing that's not based on driving but walking, and everything is a 10-minute walk, not an hour drive. The sociological impact of that book was quite astonishing to me, which was an enormous resentment of the Newport community – and tells the story of Newport - that someone who'd just moved there, would do a guidebook to their city they had lived in for so long. So it wasn't very well received by many of the Bellevue Avenue citizenry.

Although later, the second edition of it was co-published with the Preservation Society of Newport County, the backbone of that community, and that sort of turned the tables of resentment because their endorsement was the fundamental historic endorsement of the town. The first edition was shaky, the second edition was received better. My second favorite city at that time, and very much a sister city to Newport, was Charleston, where I started doing my TEDMED conferences in 1995. I thought I'd be doing them in Charleston for a long time, so I may as well have a guidebook for myself. All these things are indulgent projects I do so I can have them, and there wasn't a good guidebook to Charleston, so I did one, same as in Newport.

RSW

NEWPORT

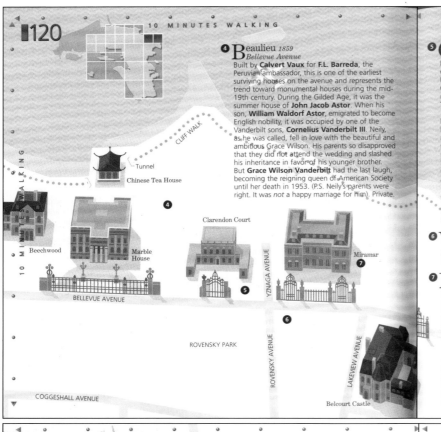

④ Beaulieu *1859*
Bellevue Avenue
Built by **Calvert Vaux** for **F.L. Barreda**, the Peruvian ambassador, this is one of the earliest surviving houses on the avenue and represents the trend toward monumental houses during the mid-19th century. During the Gilded Age, it was the summer house of **John Jacob Astor**. When his son, **William Waldorf Astor**, emigrated to become English nobility, it was occupied by one of the Vanderbilt sons, **Cornelius Vanderbilt III**. Neily, as he was called, fell in love with the beautiful and ambitious Grace Wilson. His parents so disapproved that they did not attend the wedding and slashed his inheritance in favor of his younger brother. But **Grace Wilson Vanderbilt** had the last laugh, becoming the reigning queen of American Society until her death in 1953. (P.S. Neily's parents were right. It was *not* a happy marriage for him). Private.

⑤ Clarendon Court *1904*
Bellevue Avenue at Rovensky
In 1956, Hollywood showcased this house as the epitome of American *High Society*—remember **Bing Crosby** and **Grace Kelly** singing *True Love*? (Sigh). Well, the darker side of a fairytale social marriage was also enacted at this **Horace Trumbauer** mansion. Here, just before Christmas 1980, the beautiful heiress, **Martha Sunny Von Bulow**, slipped into an irreversible coma. Her husband, **Claus Von Bulow**, was accused of attempted murder and, in a 1982 Newport court, was found guilty. The scandalous case made a media circus of Newport and bitterly split the Summer Colony. The verdict was overturned later in Providence when Von Bulow was represented by **Alan Dershowitz**. The accused now lives abroad. *That* movie, *Reversal of Fortune*, was not filmed at Clarendon Court. The house, modeled on a 1710 English manorhouse was originally built for Pennsylvania Railroad executive, **Edward C. Knight**. Private.

⑥ Weetamoe *Thayer Cottage 1870*
Bellevue Avenue at Rovensky
A vivid example of the stick style wooden villa. Private.

⑦ Miramar *1914*
Bellevue Avenue
The last of **Horace Trumbauer**'s massive neoclassical Newport houses, Miramar was built for the **George Wideners** of Philadelphia. Mr. Widener and his son were among those lost on the **Titanic** in 1912. Private.

The Almighty Dollar: How Much Did it Cost?

It's actually very difficult to measure the purchasing power of a Gilded Age dollar against a dollar today. Scholars we consulted gave us 1890 to 1990 comparison figures from as high as $33 to $1, to a moderate $22 to $1, to a conservative $14 to $1.

For the cost of goods, we decided to go with the most conservative figure, which was developed by Professor of History Maury Klein of the University of Rhode Island in consultation with the economists at Forbes magazine. So a house like Marble House, constructed and furnished at an estimated cost of $11 million between 1888 and 1892, would cost at least $154 million today—assuming you could reproduce it! These were the days when a dozen eggs were 21 cents, butter 25 cents a pound, a whole case of fine French bordeaux wine under $8 and a ton of good grade heating coal for $4. And, yes, good cigars were 5 cents! A man could buy good leather shoes for $5, a bicycle for $20 and an elegant beaver coat for $14, while the best ladies' corset was a mere 62 cents and cashmere gloves were 50 cents a pair. However, when we look at the cost of services, the higher comparative figure of $33 to $1 is actually more accurate! If you were the mistress or master of a grand Newport mansion in 1890, you could hire the finest French chef for $110 a month (about $3630 today), a proper English butler for $63 a month (now about $2,079), and a footman or a gardener for about $1 a day (try hiring a gardener for $33 a day these days!). Help was so cheap and wages so low that it's easy to see why life was so very grand indeed for those in the upper classes. In 1890, a nice little cottage by the sea might rent for $750 for the whole summer. But you could lease a very elegant large house on Bellevue Avenue or Narragansett Avenue for $2,000 to $5,000 for the 10-week summer season, and you could buy a modern 22-room house on 5,000 square feet along the older section of Bellevue (city water, gas and a stables!) for only $8,000. But a High Society family summering for those 10 weeks would likely spend more than $100,000 to $200,000 during that period! Some top-echelon families set aside as much as $300,000 (per season) for entertaining alone, while one hostess sighed that she earmarked $10,000 every summer for mistakes in my clothes. A single social event—food, wine, orchestra, extra servants—could easily cost a family upwards of $70,000 (hmmm, times 14, that's a mere $980,000 today...).

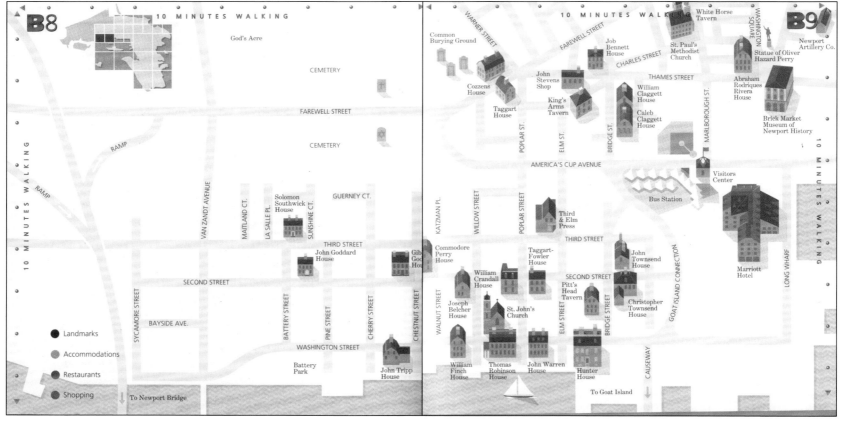

- ● Landmarks
- ● Accommodations
- ● Restaurants
- ● Shopping

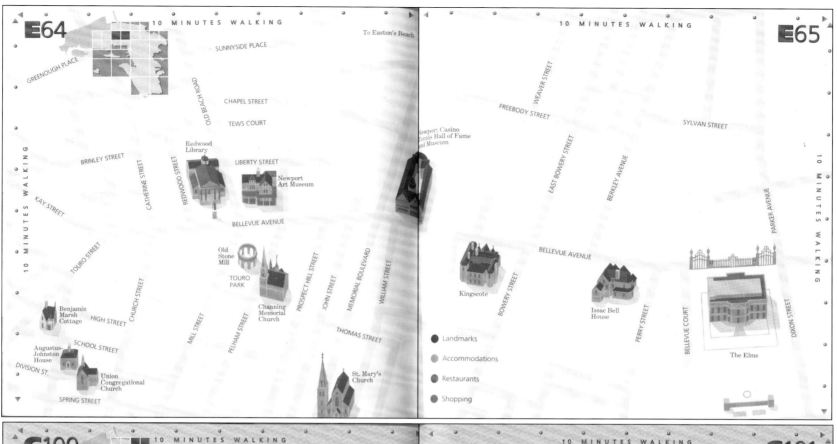

To Easton's Beach

SUNNYSIDE PLACE

GREENOUGH PLACE

OLD BEACH ROAD

CHAPEL STREET

TEWS COURT

BRINLEY STREET

KAY STREET

CATHERINE STREET

REDWOOD STREET

Redwood Library

LIBERTY STREET

Newport Art Museum

BELLEVUE AVENUE

TOURO STREET

CHURCH STREET

HIGH STREET

Old Stone Mill

TOURO PARK

Channing Memorial Church

PROSPECT HILL STREET

JOHN STREET

MEMORIAL BOULEVARD

WILLIAM STREET

Benjamin Marsh Cottage

SCHOOL STREET

MILL STREET

PELHAM STREET

Augustus-Johnston House

DIVISION ST.

Union Congregational Church

SPRING STREET

THOMAS STREET

St. Mary's Church

Newport Casino Tennis Hall of Fame and Museum

WEAVER STREET

FREEBODY STREET

SYLVAN STREET

EAST BOWERY STREET

BERKLEY AVENUE

PARKER AVENUE

BELLEVUE AVENUE

Kingscote

BOWERY STREET

Issac Bell House

PERRY STREET

BELLEVUE COURT

DIXON STREET

The Elms

● Landmarks
● Accommodations
● Restaurants
● Shopping

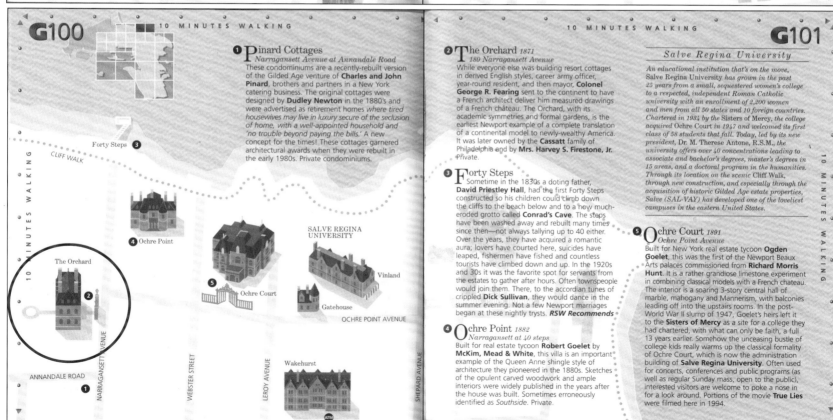

CLIFF WALK

Forty Steps ❸

❹ Ochre Point

SALVE REGINA UNIVERSITY

The Orchard

❺ Ochre Court

Vinland

Gatehouse

OCHRE POINT AVENUE

NARRAGANSETT AVENUE

ANNANDALE ROAD

WEBSTER STREET

LEROY AVENUE

Wakehurst

SHEPARD AVENUE

❶ ❷

ATM

❶ Pinard Cottages
Narragansett Avenue at Annandale Road
These condominiums are a recently-rebuilt version of the Gilded Age venture of **Charles and John Pinard**, brothers and partners in a New York catering business. The original cottages were designed by **Dudley Newton** in the 1880's and were advertised as retirement homes *where tired housewives may live in luxury secure of the seclusion of home, with a well-appointed household and 'no trouble beyond paying the bills.'* A new concept for the times! These cottages garnered architectural awards when they were rebuilt in the early 1980s. Private condominiums.

❷ The Orchard *1871*
180 Narragansett Avenue
While everyone else was building resort cottages in derived English styles, career army officer, year-round resident, and then mayor, **Colonel George R. Fearing** sent to the continent to have a French architect deliver him measured drawings of a French château. The Orchard, with its academic symmetries and formal gardens, is the earliest Newport example of a complete translation of a continental model to newly-wealthy America. It was later owned by the **Cassatt** family of Philadelphia and by **Mrs. Harvey S. Firestone, Jr.** Private.

❸ Forty Steps
Sometime in the 1830s a doting father, **David Priestley Hall**, had the first Forty Steps constructed so his children could climb down the cliffs to the beach below and to a now much-eroded grotto called **Conrad's Cave**. The steps have been washed away and rebuilt many times since then—not always tallying up to 40 either. Over the years, they have acquired a romantic aura; lovers have courted here, suicides have leaped, fishermen have fished and countless tourists have climbed down and up. In the 1920s and 30s it was the favorite spot for servants from the estates to gather after hours. Often townspeople would join them. There, to the accordian tunes of crippled **Dick Sullivan**, they would dance in the summer evening. Not a few Newport marriages began at these nightly trysts. *RSW Recommends*

❹ Ochre Point *1882*
Narragansett at 40 steps
Built for real estate tycoon **Robert Goelet** by **McKim, Mead & White**, this villa is an important example of the Queen Anne shingle style of architecture they pioneered in the 1880s. Sketches of the opulent carved woodwork and ample interiors were widely published in the years after the house was built. Sometimes erroneously identified as *Southside*. Private.

Salve Regina University

An educational institution that's on the move, Salve Regina University has grown in the past 25 years from a small, sequestered women's college to a respected, independent Roman Catholic university with an enrollment of 2,200 women and men from all 50 states and 10 foreign countries. Chartered in 1934 by the Sisters of Mercy, the college acquired Ochre Court in 1947 and welcomed its first class of 58 students that fall. Today, led by its new president, Dr. M. Therese Antone, R.S.M., the university offers over 40 concentrations leading to associate and bachelor's degrees, master's degrees in 15 areas, and a doctoral program in the humanities. Through its location on the scenic Cliff Walk, through new construction, and especially through the acquisition of historic Gilded Age estate properties, Salve (SAL-VAY) has developed one of the loveliest campuses in the eastern United States.

❺ Ochre Court *1891*
Ochre Point Avenue
Built for New York real estate tycoon **Ogden Goelet**, this was the first of the Newport Beaux Arts palaces commissioned from **Richard Morris Hunt**. It is a rather grandiose limestone experiment in combining classical models with a French chateau. The interior is a soaring 3-story central hall of marble, mahogany and Mannerism, with balconies leading off into the upstairs rooms. In the post-World War II slump of 1947, Goelet's heirs left it to the **Sisters of Mercy** as a site for a college they had chartered, with what can only be faith, a full 13 years earlier. Somehow the unceasing bustle of college kids really warms up the classical formality of Ochre Court, which is now the administration building of **Salve Regina University**. Often used for concerts, conferences and public programs (as well as regular Sunday mass, open to the public), interested visitors are welcome to poke a nose in for a look around. Portions of the movie **True Lies** were filmed here in 1994.

CHARLESTON

27 Photo Express
106 North Market Street
One-hour film development, disposable cameras, repairs, and photo accessories. M-Sa 9AM-6PM, Su 10AM-5PM. Tel 723.3833 or 723.3840.

28 Cosmic Charlie's
104 North Market Street
Exotic jewelry and incense.

29 Chef and Clef ss
102 North Market Street
Serious live jazz and blues accompany your drinks or dinner in this movin' little club. People come here to listen rather than eat, so the food is more of an afterthought. However, you can order *eighth notes* like Crab Stuffed Mushrooms or Almond Crusted Brie or, if seriously hungry, go on up to *whole notes* like Charbroiled Salmon or Bourbon Street Seafood Fettucine and enjoy the music you came to Charleston to hear. Nightly 6PM-4AM. Dancing and romancing till the wee hours begins at 9:30PM on the 3rd floor in **The Red Hot Blues Room**. A good **Jazz Brunch** is served from 11AM each Sunday—and they give you 10% off the price if you show up with a church bulletin! Tel 722.0732.

30 Market Street Sweets
100 North Market Street
Pralines, fudge, fresh chocolate. They do gifts and baskets as well. Tel 722.1397.

31 Scents Unlimited
92 North Market Street AM
Affordable fragrances. Su-Th 10-9PM, F-Sa 10AM-10PM. Tel 853.8837.

32 Aspen Bay Trading Co.
90 North Market Street
Rugged casual wear. Tel 722.4216.

33 Madeline's Lingerie
88 North Market Street
Intimate apparel, both naughty and nice. Tel 723.0087.

34 Market Arts Gallery
86 North Market Street
Souvenir art.

35 Shops at 84 North Market, including:

Fun Thinkers
84 North Market Street
For the kids on your list and the plain old young at heart, toys and nifty gifts. Tel 720.8697.

B & E Estate Jewelers
84 North Market Street
Interesting jewelry, previously owned. Tel 853.0183.

Quackers
84 North Market Street
Souvenirs. Tel 722.2889.

Sheila's Shamrock
84 North Market Street
Crafts and gifts. Tel 577.0833.

36 T-Bonz Gill & Grill ss
80 North Market Street
T-Bonz's motto—*There's no such thing as an 'OK' steak*—should tell you you're in for some seriously fine beef. The menu is just what it says—good steaks, good local seafood. Environmentally conscious, they don't use preservatives or sulfides and do some serious recycling. T-Bonz also has a full bar with a big variety of brews on tap. (**Kaminisky's Cafe** is right next door for the big finish dessert!) Late nights, T-Bonz is a *major watering hole* for the young and glamorous. From 11 AM daily. Tel 577.2511.

37 Kaminsky's Excellent Café s.ss
78 North Market Street
How true, how true! Kaminsky's is *most* excellent and you just can't visit Charleston without a stop here. **Divine desserts**, coffees, full bar, and an impressive wine list, served by the glass. They also serve the city's **Best Milkshake**—heavenly on a hot afternoon. The atmosphere is inviting, the staff is truly pleasant, and the calories are worth every guilty bite. Charlestonians will often forego dessert with dinner to finish their evening here, as Kaminsky's is open very late. You can also get your sinful portion to go—by the whole or the slice—so you just can't say *no*. Daily from noon to whenever. Tel 853.8270.
RSW recommends

38 Peanut Shop of Charleston
76 North Market Street
Tel 723.6052.

39 Materialistic
74 North Market Street
Crafts and gifts from Africa, the Caribbean, and other exotic venues. Tel 853.2525.

40 ABC's by Lucy
72 North Market Street
Alphabet art. Tel 722.5974.

41 Mistral ss
99 South Market Street
Francoise Duffy, a native of Nice, is hostess and owner of this spot which offers cozy country French ambiance and a happy marriage between classic French food and local fare. Fresh-baked bread perfumes the air, Provençal tablecloths are spread, Toulouse-Lautrec lithos are on the walls and *real* she-crab soup is on the menu. The noisette is Mahi-Mahi, the poultry is likely to be Carolina Quail, stuffed with vidalia onions and andouille sausage as well as veal, beef, and seafood. Beginning at 9PM, Th-Sa, **Mistral** forsakes the quaint French background music for live Dixieland jazz. Lunch, Dinner from 11AM, closed Sun. night. Tel 722.5708.

42 Market Street Mill s.ss
99 Market Street
Charleston now has its own brew pub which styles itself as a bakery, eatery, brewery. Their original beers are intriguing—*Market Street Amber, Port City Porter, Eureka Honey Wheat, Ice House Schooner Lager.* You can try a sampler of 5 for pocket change or take home a liter of draft beer to go for $9. There's something to appeal to everyone like Grilled Tuna Steak on cheddar roll with Stir-fry Veggies or Meatloaf Pasta. Besides lunch and dinner, they serve breakfast—try the Jack Daniels's Chocolate Cheesecake for breakfast (feel happy all day!). Or (on the lighter side) sample the airy and delectable home-baked muffins. Daily 8AM - 2AM. Tel 722.6100.

75 The Gingko Leaf
159 King Street
Specializing in decorative antiques, combining dried flower arrangements and topiary with intriguing artifacts. M-Sa 10AM-5:30PM. Tel 724.0640.

76 Elizabeth Lyle Gallery
161 King Street
Specializing in decoys, paintings and prints of wildlife. M-Sa 10AM-5:30PM. Tel 723.2600.

77 Moore House Antiques
161 1/2 King Street
American furniture, Chinese porcelain, and early 19th century china. M-Sa 10AM-5:30PM. Tel 722.8065.

78 Livingston & Sons Antiques, Inc.
163 King Street
The Livingstons are direct importers from England and the continent. The fine furniture and fascinating collectibles here are just the tip of the iceberg. They keep a warehouse and run regular auctions. M-Sa 10AM-6PM. Tel 723.9697.

79 Charleston Library Society 1914
164 King Street
In 1748, a group of gentlemen interested in the philosophical and scientific issues of their day founded the **Charleston Library Society**, the third oldest private library of its kind in America. The founders insisted that they did it to *save their descendents from sinking into savagery!* (You be the judge.) After many years on Broad Street, this building was erected in 1914. Members and their guests only. Tel 723.9912.

The Gateway Walk

Developed and maintained by the Charleston Garden Club, the Gateway Walk passes through here, south of the Charleston Library Society and south of the Gibbes Museum of Art. By using this appealing pedestrian lane, you can stroll all the way from the cemeteries of the Unitarian and Lutheran churches on Archdale Street to the doors of St. Philip's Episcopal Church on Church Street.

80 Elizabeth Austin Antiques
165 King Street
This shop is full of exquisite antique silver. Also estate and antique jewelry. M-Sa 10AM-5PM. Tel 722. 0248.

81 Helen S. Martin Antiques
169 King Street
Ivory, figurines, steins, books, antique firearms—many small, curious, wonderful items. M-Sa 9AM-5PM. Tel 577.6533.

82 Charlie's
173 King Street
This tiny grocery sells beer and wine as well as snacks. Tel 722.3068.

83 Poppe House
177 King Street
Antiques and good quality reproductions in mahogany. Mantels, moldings and other architectural accessories. M-Sa 10AM-5:30PM. Tel 853.9559.

84 Decorator's Alley
177 1/2 King Street
Down an alley into a walled courtyard and up the stairs. Some is junk, but some interesting lamps, mirrors, objets d'art. Tel 722.2707.

85 English Patina
179 King Street
This very small shop houses a big selection of directly imported English and European 18th and 19th century furniture. M-Sa 10AM-5PM. Tel 853.0380.

86 D. Bigda Antiques
178 King Street
Estate jewelry and vintage watches. Bigda has a large inventory of sterling holloware and can help you with pattern matching. David and Daisy Bigda LOVE silver and are especially helpful in identifying esoteric silver objects and pieces. M-Sa 10AM-5PM. Tel 722.0248.

87 Jack Patla Co.
181 King Street
Fire andirons, garden fixtures, silver. Tel 723.2314.

88 John Gibson Antiques
183 King Street
Solid mahogany reproduction furniture of good quality. Custom orders accepted. Tel 722.0909.

89 Charleston Florist, Inc.
184 1/2 King Street
Excellent floral designs from a family business, including fresh flowers and silk. You can send flowers worldwide. Tel 577.7599.

90 Joint Ventures Estate Jewelers
185 King Street
This is an excellent consignment shop for silver flatware and holloware, jewelry and timepieces. Prices are good. M-Sa 10AM-5PM. Tel 722.6730.

91 RTW Ltd.
186 King Street
The couture of this elegant women's clothing store is *très haute* indeed. Many of the unique, high-fashion garments seem to have stepped right off the runway of some of the great design houses. The collections from Italy, France, Belgium, and the U.S. allow a discriminating shopper to create wardrobes from the everyday (first floor) to black tie and formal (special occasion dressing is upstairs). There are some very fine one-of-a-kind offerings—I bought two beautiful scarves here. **Janyce McMenamin** and her attentive, professional staff are there to help you. M-Sa 10AM-5PM. Tel 577.9748. **RSW recommends**

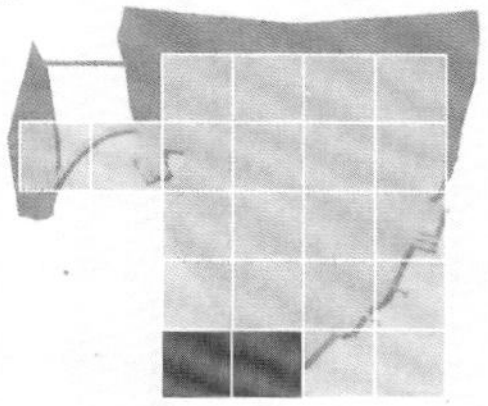

(left vertical margin)

8 Courtney House *c. 1855*
11 Meeting Street
Sometime between 1850 and 1860 **William Courtney** built this large stuccoed brick house in the Italianate style. Private.

9 Calhoun Mansion *1876*
16 Meeting Street
With most of the city impoverished in the two decades following the end of the Civil War, few grand new houses were built in Charleston. But **George Walton Williams**, who had made a fortune in groceries before the war, came through the war with more than $1 million in capital assets. After the war he became Charleston's most successful banker, founding the **Carolina Savings Bank** in 1874. When he came to build a mansion for himself and his family, Williams spared no expense, spending more than $200,000 on this magnificent house designed by **William P. Russell**—the equivalent of over $2.8 million today (assuming you could reproduce it). With more than 24,000 square feet of living space, this house was then (and is still today) the **largest single residence in the city**. From the rooftop cupola, over 80 feet above the street, there is a sweeping view of the harbor. The brick mansion has 35 rooms elegantly

elaborated in paneled walnut and satinwood, molded plaster ceilings, and walls with hand-painted scenes. The music room or ballroom is breathtaking, rising 45 feet to a coved glass skylight. Williams' son-in-law, **Patrick Calhoun** (grandson of the Great Nullifier) was the next owner. After World War I, the house became a hotel named for him, **The Calhoun Mansion**. In 1976-77 this important Victorian residence was lovingly and meticulously restored by owners **Dianne and Gedney M. Howe III**. It, along with the Joseph Manigault House and the Edmondston Alston House are featured in the television series *America's Castles*. W-Su 10AM-4PM. Fee. *Tel 722.8205.* **RSW recommends**

10 John Edwards House *1770*
15 Meeting Street
The prominent **John Edwards**, who served in John Rutledge's Privy Council, built his house with some touches of grandeur. Both the stuccoed basement and the cypress wood of the facade have been rusticated (cut and beveled to resemble more expensive stone). The Corinthian columned portico has an impressive double flight of stairs. The Georgian interior details are exceptional. Edwards was one of the group of 60 prominent Patriots exiled to St. Augustine in 1780. The British lost no time in commandeering the house to quarter **Admiral Arbuthnot**. The family of the **Comte de Grasse** was sheltered here by Edwards' son-in-law when they were refugees from the 1793 Santo Domingo Revolution. In the late 19th century **George Williams Jr.** (son of the city's most prominent banker who lived at **#16**) added the oversized semicircular piazza on the south side of the house. Tradition has it that it was constructed in this fashion so that it could accomodate all the children from the **Charleston Orphan House**

for frequent ice cream parties. Note the large ginko trees which are absolutely spectacular in autumn! Private.

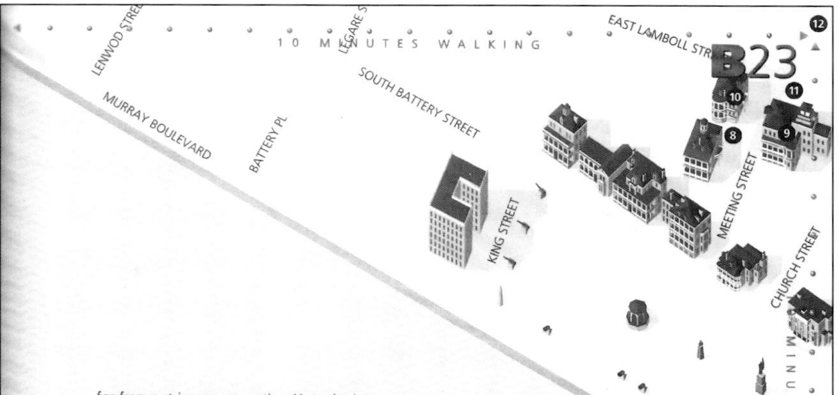

11 Heyward House *1803*
18 Meeting Street
One of the **Heyward brothers** built this fine Adamesque single house just after the turn of the 19th century, but it is unknown if it was Nathaniel or Thomas (who signed the Declaration of Independence). There is a secret room, apparently a wine closet, on the second floor. A later owner, **James Adger**, operated the first coastal steamship line in the U.S. Private.

12 William Mason Smith House
c. 1822 26 Meeting Street
This very formal Regency style house was built by the son of South Carolina's first Episcopal Bishop. Notice that the piazza, masked by masonry and windows, has the correct order of architecture—Doric, Ionic, and Corinthian, in ascending sequence. Private.

Charleston Cliches

You will hear some version of each of these old saws if you stay in town for more than a few days:

"Charlestonians are like the Chinese. They eat rice, worship their ancestors and speak an unintelligible language."

"Broad Street is the dividing line between longing and belonging."

"A man born South of Broad Street who is a member of the St. Cecilia Society and of St. Michael's Church is guaranteed a seat in heaven, but probably won't want to go."

One born in Charleston is "from here." Any other Southerner is "from away." Northerners, Westerners and other foreigners are "from off."

When the Ashley and the Cooper Rivers join at the foot of the Charleston Peninsula, they form the Atlantic Ocean.

The Civil War and Reconstruction left Charleston "Too poor to paint, too proud to whitewash."

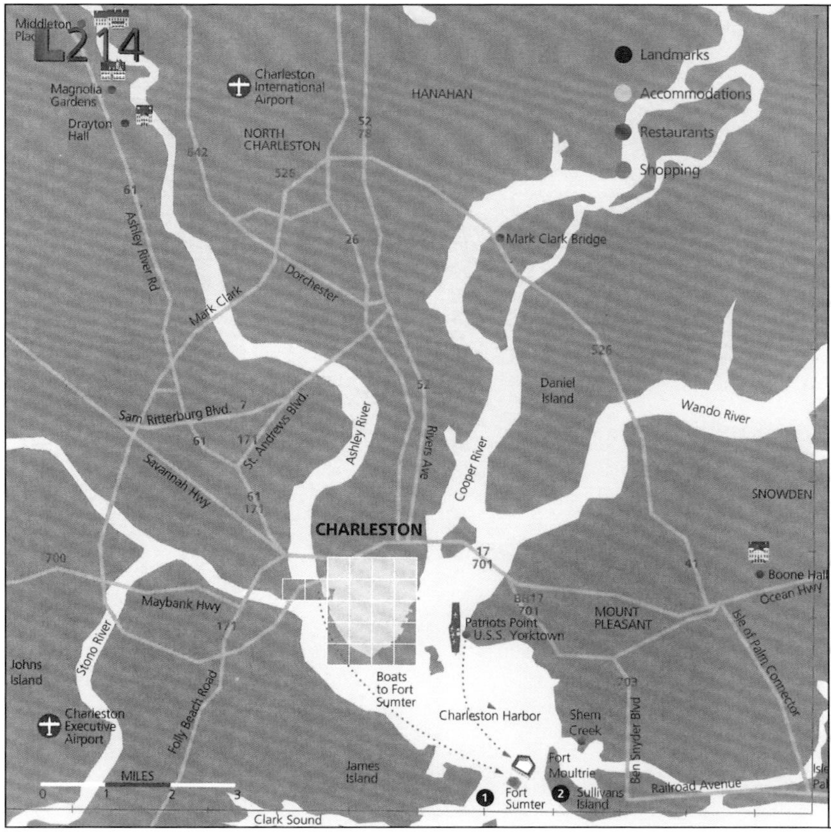

1 Fort Sumter *begun 1829, never completed entrance to Charleston Harbor*
This is one of those rare historic sites where so many things you vaguely remember from your elementary school history lessons suddenly become vivid and immediate. This small fort, stuck out on a pile of rocks in the harbor, still within sight of Charleston, was in the pre-dawn hours of April 12, 1861 the flashpoint at which the American Civil War ignited. After a two-day bombardment, **U.S. Army Major Robert Anderson** and his 85 men surrendered the fort to South Carolina forces and the dreaded war was underway. From April 1861 to February 1865, Fort Sumter was a symbol of Confederate determination. The troops defending it went through one of the longest sieges in modern warfare, experiencing almost two years of bombardment by an estimated 46,000 shells (about 7 million pounds of metal). It is now a *National Monument*, staffed by the **U.S. Park Service** (of which I am a big fan!). Many boat tours will take you by the fort, but *only* **Fort Sumter Tours** dock for the tour. **Boat tours** leave from **Charleston's City Marina** and from **Patriots Point in Mt. Pleasant**. The comfortable voyage each way takes about 35 minutes, while you have an hour at the fort. The trip out is a good way to see a bit of the harbor, with sights along the riverside and along **the Battery** pointed out. There's a good historical narrative piped in—precise and informative, but not intrusive. At the fort you can self-guide by using the free interpretive map and the on-site markers. One of the Park Rangers also offers a lively, amusing historical mini-lecture—optional, but worth the few minutes. When you've wandered among the ruins of the enlisted men's barracks, squinted along a Civil War cannon, and watched the pelicans flock on the shallow mud flats, *be sure to* go inside and do the air-conditioned **museum**, renovated in 1994. The excellent exhibits include 3-dimensional models and maps, terrific period photographs and newspapers, and the two original flags of the battle, the Stars and Stripes of the United States and the Palmetto Flag of South Carolina—all well-interpreted. They give a feeling for Charleston during the conflict, as well as of the

defenses of the fort. The gift shop has lots of Confederate mementos and books. (No snack bar.) Daily, tour hours available vary with the time of year. Be sure to check. April 1- Labor Day 9:30AM-4PM. Fee (children under 6 FREE).*Tel 722.6191.* **RSW Recommends**

2 Fort Moultrie *1776, 1809*
1213 Middle Street, Sullivan's Island
Part of the **Fort Sumter National Monument, Fort Moultrie** is an historic point of coastal defense that goes all the way back to the Revolution. In 1776, the fort was just a pen of palmetto logs piled with sand when the invading British in a fleet of 9 man o' war ships with 300 guns attacked the crude fort and its 400 defenders. But the British hadn't reckoned on those spongy palmetto logs! Basically, the shots were absorbed by the palmetto logs or were smothered in the sand before they could explode. The British actually retreated and didn't take Charleston for another 3 years. The flag of South Carolina has flown the palmetto tree ever since and the fort was named for commanding officer **Col. William Moultrie**. This fort is the 1809 version, but a tour here (either guided or self-guided with **U.S. Park Service** materials) will take you right through U.S. military history of coastal defense. Among the famous who have served here are writer **Edgar Allen Poe** (who used the setting in *The Gold Bug*), **General William T. Sherman** (Union commander who marched through the South, with devastating results) and **General George C. Patton** (who became Army Chief of Staff within 6 years). You'll find the grave here of **Osceola**, the Seminole Indian chief. There are paths right down to the beach here and the jetty is a superb place to watch ocean-going ships slip out of the harbor to the sea. The two visible lighthouses are **Morris Island Light** (to the far right, 1767, 1870) and **Sullivan's Island Light** (far left, 1960). Daily 9AM-5PM FREE. *Tel 883.3123.*
Harbor Tours and Tours of Fort Sumter
Daily regular departures from Patriots Point, plenty of parking.

Jack Dangermond

> *Knowing where things are, and why, is essential to rational decision making.*

JACK DANGERMOND

> *Don't ever walk by a wilting plant. Get water on it right away.*

JACK DANGERMOND

73

CHAPTER CREDIT
Jack Dangermond
Clint Brown
Christian Harder

Geography is just physics slowed down, with a couple of trees stuck in it.

TERRY PRATCHETT

A map is the greatest of all epic poems. It's lines and colors show the realization of great dreams.

GILBERT H. GROSVENOR

Man is a blind, witless, low brow, anthropocentric clod which inflicts lesions upon the Earth.

IAN MCHARG

Coming back to where you started is not the same as leaving.

TERRY PRATCHETT

SEEING LEADS TO UNDERSTANDING
GIS technology combines maps with data so you can see the world in a smarter way. With converging advances in live data, 3D graphics, cloud computing, and mobile technology, GIS applications provide rich immersive experiences like this planning scenario app for Los Angeles, California.

GIS - UNDERSTANDING THE SCIENCE OF WHERE

GIS is a tool for integration and unerstanding; Maps and geography provide the fundamental language for understanding and together they provide a framework for organizing and communicating our knowledge. Increasingly maps are used in every field, providing a universal language for communicating ideas and insights.

People are visual learners and seem to be instinctively attracted to maps. Maps help humans instantly perceive patterns, relationships and situations. They not only organize and present the rich content of our world, they offer a unique contextual framework for understanding, predicting and designing the future.

Maps and data provide the underpinnings of GIS. In turn, GIS organizes information into all types of layers that can be visualized, analyzed and combined to help us understand everything. Seeing things on a map helps you make better decisions. That's what GIS is all about.

GIS is attractive to most people who encounter it because it is both intuitive and cognitive. It combines powerful mapping and visualization with a strong data integration, analysis and modeling framework that is rooted in the science of geography.

GIS has a unique capability to integrate many kinds of data. It uses spatial location and digital map overlays to organize the content of our world. These overlays can be used to integrate and analyze relationships between all types of data. This combination has resulted in a powerful analytic technology that is science-based, trusted and easily communicated using maps and other forms of geographic visualization.

EARLY HISTORY OF GIS

THE ACADEMY

The field of GIS got its start in the 1960s as computers and early concepts of quantitative and computational geography began to emerge. This early work included important research by the academic community with many notable contributions by scholars and researchers such as Duane Marble, David Bickmore, Waldo Tobler, Carl Steinitz, Ed Horwood and William Garrison. Later, the National Center for Geographic Information and Analysis (NCGIA), led by Michael Goodchild, formalized research on key geographic information science topics such as spatial analysis, visualization and the representation of uncertainty. These efforts fueled a quantitative

EXISTING

SCENARIO PLA

Single Family
Multi-family
Town house
Mixed-Use Residential
Office
Retail
Public
Industry

rio Planning
hat parcel

3 User scenario plan

[Scenario Planning
+ CE] python tool

4 Enhanced user plan
with 3D features

[Add reference]
Python tool

Excel macros button

5 SED comparison (user
plan to policy goals)

6 Updated Scenario
Planning report / ROI
model

F.A.R

9.8	Office 30
5.1	Office 15
4.8	Mixed-Use Residential 15
2.6	Mixed-Use Residential 5
	Main Street Retail LifeStyle

Difference after enhanced with CityEng

Population
24,747   7%

Job
9,152   26%

Property Tax Revenue
$2,100,000
Sales Tax Revenue
$3,450,000

Displacement population
998
Displacement value
$110,600,000

Energy Use
68 household
15

Water Consumption
215
per household

Carbon Emission
5.4
per household   8%

Solid Waste
6.0 per household
3.6 per job

Olympic Blvd.

Over Plan Zone

SAMPLE PLACE:
MID-CITY,
LOS ANGELES
CALIFORNIA

Western Ave.

gies (ArcGIS Pro and
ite of tools intends to
grams that related to
d air quality).

75

ROGER TOMLINSON

A young Roger Tomlinson at ease in 1962 as the world's first-ever computerized GIS operations run on the IBM System/360 behind him. For this work, he is recognized as the Father of GIS.

We are bullies of the Earth: strong, foul, coarse, greedy, careless, indifferent to others, laying waste as we proceed, leaving wounds, welts, lesions, suppurations on the Earth body, increasingly engulfed by our own ordure and, finally, abysmally ignorant of the way the world works, crowing our superiority over all life.

TERRY PRATCHETT

revolution in the world of geographic science and strengthened the foundation of GIS. The concept of GIS began in earnest in the 1960s. Dr. Roger Tomlinson was the first to give GIS its name. His pioneering work to initiate, plan, and direct the development of the Canada Geographic Information System resulted in the first computerized GIS in the world. The Canadian government had launched a national program to inventory and manage its natural resources. Dr. Tomlinson envisioned the use of computers to bring all of this data together for natural resources across all provinces. He had an idea that the new automated mainframe computer technologies from IBM might be applicable, and even necessary, to complete such a detail-oriented task more effectively and efficiently than humans could achieve manually. He created the design for automated computing to store and process large amounts of data, which enabled Canada to begin a national land-use management program and become an early promoter and pioneer of geographic information systems—the beginning of GIS.

1965: THE HARVARD LABORATORY FOR COMPUTER GRAPHICS

While at Northwestern University in 1964, Howard Fisher created one of the first computer mapping software programs, known as SYMAP. In 1965, he established the Harvard Laboratory for Computer Graphics and Spatial Analysis. This laboratory not only created and refined some of the first computer mapmaking software, it also became a research center for spatial analysis and visualization. Fisher created an environment where people had the freedom to explore new ideas, and explore they did. Many of the early concepts for GIS and its applications were conceived at the Lab.

The Lab attracted a talented collection of geographers, planners, computer scientists, and others from many fields who invented and synthesized some of the modern concepts that underpin computer mapping and spatial analysis.

ESRI/THE COMPANY

In 1969 we started Esri as a small company to apply computer mapping and spatial analysis to land use and environmental problem solving. Our early projects used primitive software tools, but this early work was already demonstrating the tremendous value of using a GIS approach.

Back then, we had begun to realize that all types of geographic information could be put into the computer as overlays to analyze complex problems. The experience that we gained from our early projects prompted us to develop many of the methods now in use. These results generated an interest in our software tools and workflows that are now a standard part of a GIS.

JACK DANGERMOND
Redlands, CA circa 1970

Over time as computing became more powerful and affordable, we incrementally improved our software tools to support our project work. Working on real-world problems not only helped our customers make better decisions, but also led us to innovate and develop robust GIS tools and approachTes. The result of this work eventually gained acceptance and recognition as a new way of doing spatial analysis and planning.

This work led to the creation of our commercial GIS product known as Arc/Info. This technology was first released in 1981 and began the evolution of Esri into a software company. Our mapping and analysis software amplified understanding by leveraging geospatial knowledge and making it visible for everyone.

Our initial product enabled each user to apply our software and methods to create their own digital map layers and do GIS-related applications much as we had done in our consulting practice. Over time our users not only created data and did their own projects, they also began to share and collaborate with each other. We started to envision that, collectively, our users' work could form a continuous, overlapping, and interoperable GIS database for the world—about virtually all subjects. With this vision, GIS users—and ultimately, all of humanity—would be able to access and leverage this powerful system to address practically any kind of issue or problem we face. This vision not only transformed our organization but also launched a whole new GIS industry. Looking back, we realized that we were engaged with other contributors in creating a whole new approach for understanding and using GIS.

Fast forward to today, this vision is rapidly becoming a reality enabled by cloud computing and the Internet. Literally hundreds of thousands of organizations are now sharing their work with billions of maps being created and used every day. These maps not only tell stories, they can be overlaid, combined, and analyzed to help us understand patterns and relationships about everything in the world.

1969: ENVIRONMENTAL SYSTEMS RESEARCH INSTITUTE COMES TO LIFE

I was going to school and working at the Harvard Lab when I began to grasp the power of what we now call GIS. The notion of mapping with computers was still pretty awkward. Computing was immature and not very affordable. Nevertheless, some of the early concepts of GIS were already emerging. I found this early technology to be exciting and decided to immerse myself in this new field by starting Esri and applying these ideas to real-world problem solving.

EARLY APPROACHES
One of the early approaches used to create a computer map started by manually encoding map coordinates (top) and using the key punch machine to enter the data (center). Likewise, the graphics output was also primitive. Maps were made with line printers where the technique of overprinting alphanumeric characters was used to create light to dark symbology. Each character on the computer map printout was printed based on an underlying cell value from the map (bottom).

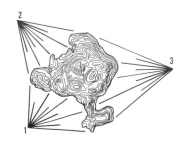

3D TOPOGRAPHIC MAPS
In 1970, working on early IBM mainframes at the University of California, Riverside, campus, Esri created one of the first 3D topographic surface maps for a proposed resort in Aizuwakamatsu, Japan (left). Today, the entire planet, including Mount Everest in Nepal (right), is mapped topographically in 3D in great detail and is accessible to anyone using a web browser or smartphone.

So in 1969, my wife Laura and I founded "Environmental Research Systems Institute" (Esri). Even from the beginning, we recognized that what was (and still is) interesting about GIS is that it can be applied broadly to many applications. This would be done by organizing data into maps and layers that could be combined and integrated to address a wide array of questions and issues.

As Esri completed more and more projects, we began to imagine that as humans we could digitize our world into layers of information that described everything. We could use the computer to overlay and analyze these layers to open up whole new ways to understand and plan our future—layers about our cities, our environment, our water and other natural resources, about potential hazards, climate and weather, transportation and infrastructure, and all about people and their characteristics.

The computing and software technology that we used in our early projects was primitive and expensive. We worked hard to develop effective and repeatable methods for applying GIS. During those early days, we were fortunate to work collaboratively with some good customers, such as the Maryland State Department of Planning, that were also interested in contributing to the practical and effective use of GIS.

The work of my colleagues at Esri (notably including software architect Scott Morehouse and product engineer Clint Brown, who led our evolution in commercial software) transformed those early concepts into GIS tools and software, building and implementing GIS applications that supported all kinds of customers the world over.

As computers have gotten better and GIS software tools have become more powerful, we have been able to advance the sophistication and reach of GIS by providing a platform to support the growing and vibrant global community of GIS practitioners.

EMERGENCE OF THE GLOBAL GIS USER COMMUNITY

As time passed, Esri grew into an influential organization that developed leading GIS software tools and applications. The approach has been to systematically integrate advancements in geographic science with ongoing innovations and the expansive growth in computing technologies. This also led to the emergence of a large and growing professional GIS community that began to apply geographic science in their work. The result has been that institutions in virtually every field and corner of the world now use our GIS software as an instrument for understanding and improving their organizations.

Today, we are starting to see where organizations everywhere are applying GIS technology to address problems at all scales. It is becoming a kind of nervous system for the planet, in which we are increasingly measuring everything that moves and changes, feeding it into the collective GIS of the World that is being used for understanding, decision making, and connecting. Geography, the science of our world, is the basis of this platform, combining all disciplines (the "-ologies") together increasingly in real time. This system is becoming a platform for all human behavior and will ultimately play a major role in the evolution of the planet.

Who could have known that, almost 50 years later, what we see today would be possible? Hundreds of thousands of organizations globally are creating their data layers about every subject. That there would be a dynamic industry with geographic information measurements from satellites, GPS, and drones. That we would live at a time when a world would emerge in which people everywhere carry location-aware phones and have become sensors as part of a global GIS, and where computing would be accessed wirelessly from our smart devices across the planet. We now occupy a world with access to GIS and map content of every type that can be integrated and analyzed. Our users, in over 350,000 organizations worldwide, build the maps that run their organizations and the world. It's actually quite a dramatic and powerful outcome from what we envisioned so long ago.

SCOTT MOREHOUSE,
Palm Springs, CA 2015.

MINICOMPUTERS
Starting in the early 1980s, Esri delivered its commercial software on minicomputers. At a cost of about $250,000 at the time, these computers had become seemingly affordable, enabling organizations to buy and operate their own hardware dedicated to GIS. Subsequent Esri software releases were implemented on UNIX workstations, then on personal computers, and now using cloud computing on the web.

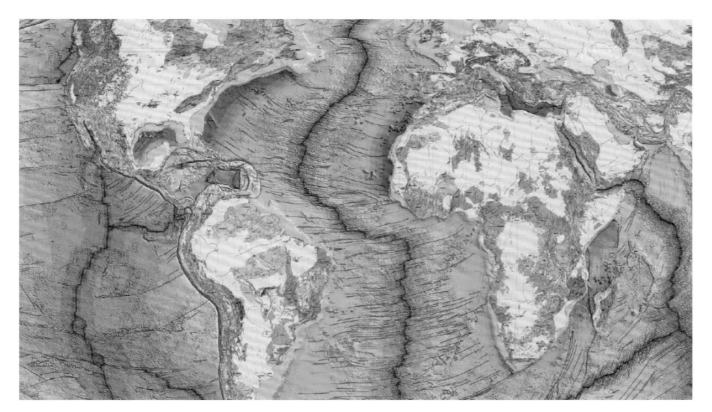

TECTONIC MAP
This digital tectonic map of Earth shows how far our understanding of the world has advanced since the first primitive digital maps created at Esri. Viewed in its proper context on a computer screen, this map becomes an interactive display that can be used to emphasize the many different geologic and geographic layers that are shown in this composite.

ARC/INFO

Arc/Info enabled organizations to digitize their own maps and data. Various maps and aerial images would be placed on a large digitizing table, similar to a drafting table. Each table had a fine electronic mesh embedded under its surface that could capture the location of the cross hairs when you clicked a button on a puck (an early precursor to the computer mouse). These tablets were used to enter coordinate locations for map features. Early GIS practitioners spent hours compiling data from map sheets, air photos, and interpreted imagery to build their GIS databases.

NETWORK ANALYSIS TOOL

An early example of a network analysis tool that continues to be used in modern GIS. This tool calculated pathways to all street segments that were closest to each facility or destination. Today, modern versions of these optimization tools are used for emergency response, school planning, retail and facility siting, and a wide array of other applications providing massive efficiencies for companies, government, and society.

THE PC

In the mid-1980s, PCs became available and affordable, dropping prices below $10,000 for computers. Commercial GIS software such as Arc/Info from Esri first began to make an appearance on these machines in dozens of implementations worldwide. This initiated the rapid growth and adoption of GIS that has continued for several decades to the broad GIS awareness that we see today.

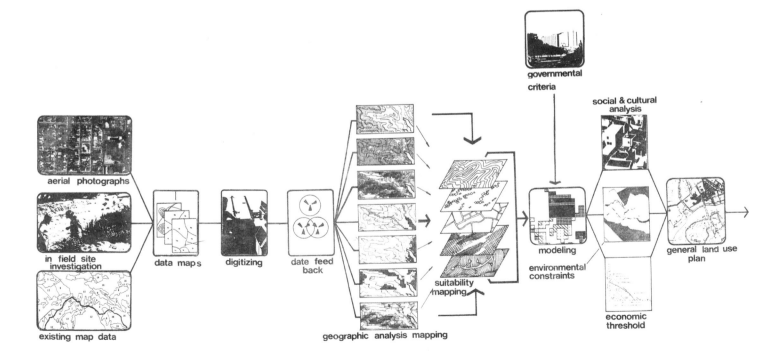

INFORMATION PLANNING SYSTEM

Diagram of the processing flow performed by Esri for the Maryland Automated Geographic Information System (MAGI) Project. This work was performed from 1972-73.

I've always been fascinated by maps and cartography. A map tells you where you've been, where you are, and where you're going - in a sense it's three tenses in one.

PETER GREENAWAY

81

INTEGRATED TERRAIN MAP OF AFRICA

One of the first comprehensive natural resource surveys of the entire African continent compiled by Esri, this **1985** Arc/Info map created for the United Nations overlaid and integrated soils, geology, landforms, slope, land use, and vegetation. The coastline was not superimposed at the time of this plot due to early software limits, so the land-water interface is not shown. This early map was used for many planning and environmental studies, including the assessment and risk of desertification. It also demonstrated the ability of GIS to handle what was, at the time, considered tobe a huge number of polygons: 48,000.

CASE STUDY: COMBATING EBOLA

In the summer of 2014, an Ebola outbreak that had been simmering in West Africa since spring suddenly exploded in numbers resulting in significant loss of life and social disruption, centered in Nigeria, Senegal, and Sierra Leone. By August of that year, the Centers for Disease Control (CDC) projected that the number of cases could top 1 million deaths by the spring of 2015.

Meanwhile, the World Health Organization (WHO) began to use GIS to gain a foothold to locate and place an amazing army of health-care workers on the ground, track existing cases and apply their response plans and activities, and anticipate where the next outbreaks would occur.

By the fall of 2014, WHO's immediate goals were to ensure 70 percent safe burials coupled with a 70 percent case isolation for new victims. They had a target to achieve these goals within 60 days. WHO applied GIS for situational awareness to coordinate, locate, and respond to new Ebola cases. It used map-based dashboards in its operations centers in Geneva and Africa to track the progress and results of each goal.

Through WHO's miraculous work and use of GIS, it had turned the epidemic around. The battle is on-going. In its communications, WHO has advised that West Africa may see further outbreaks over time.

GIS IS ABOUT UNDERSTANDING AND INSIGHTS

GIS is evolving rapidly and creating a whole new framework and process for understanding. With its simplification and deployment on the web and in cloud computing as well as its integration with real-time (IoT) information, GIS promises to become a platform relevant to almost every form of human endeavor—a nervous system for the planet. This system is now not only possible, but in many ways we believe it's inevitable. Why?

GIS integrates data about everything and at the same time is a platform for intuitively understanding this data. For scientists, this GIS nervous system will provide a framework for advancing scientific understanding, integrating and analyzing all types of spatial knowledge (all the "-ologies" such as biology, sociology, geology, climatology, and so on).

For everyone else, it will provide a platform for understanding what's going on locally and globally, a way to comprehend the complexity of our world as well as address and communicate the

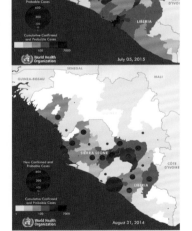

In October 2014, WHO reported an end to Ebola outbreaks in Nigeria and Senegal. Sierra Leone and Guinea both had experienced significantly larger outbreaks, and required more time. Sierra Leone was declared Ebola-free on November 7, 2015, Guinea followed in December. Liberia experienced the brunt of devastation with 4,800 deaths and close to 11,000 infections. It took until Fall 2015 for WHO to declare victory in Liberia. GIS played a major supporting role.

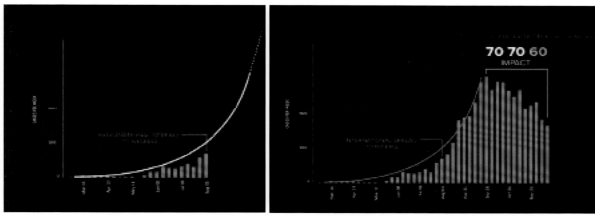

70 70 60
IMPACT

Through the WHO's miraculous work and use of GIS, within 12 months, it had turned the epidemic around. The battle is on-going. In its communications, WHO has advised that West Africa may see further outbreaks over time.

issues we face using the common language of mapping. Looking to the future, our world will increasingly be challenged with expanding population, loss of nature, environmental pollution, and the increasing dilemma of climate change and sustainability. To address these challenges, it's going to take all our best people, our most effective methodologies and technologies— scientists of many types, our best thinkers, all our best design talent collaborating to create a sustainable future.

In addition, GIS and GIS professionals will play an increasingly important role in how we address our challenges. My belief is that GIS not only helps us increase our understanding but also provides a platform for decision-making and collaboration – a platform for collective problem solving.

Richard Saul Wurman once said, *Understanding precedes action.* The evidence suggests that we need to urgently take steps to create a more sustainable future. My hope is that by using GIS, we can make better decisions and take them to action.

83

From its inception in the 1960s, GIS has gone from something that ran on a handful of computers in select research labs to a ubiquitous technology that is touched by billions of people, pretty much everywhere there are people. In this map, each dot represents a map request from a GIS user; the bigger and brighter the dots, the more the usage.

GIS IS A TOOL FOR INTEGRATION AND UNDERSTANDING

GIS is interesting because of the work that it empowers our users to do. Their projects are fascinating because they are taking on some of the biggest, most urgent problems on the planet.

The GIS examples on the following pages illustrate the extensive depth and breadth of our users' work. GIS has the extraordinary potential to reach everyone through a common visual languaage that connects people across organizations and throughout the world. Today, hundreds of thousands of organizations use GIS to make maps that communicate, perform analysis, share information and solve complex problems. This is literally changing the way the world works.

☰ M6.2 Earthquake - 10km SE of Norcia, Italy Impact Summary Map

1.4m	660k
2013 Total Population (MBR)	Total Households

Content may not reflect National Geographic's current map policy. Sources: National Geographic, Esri, DeLorme, HE...

GIS MAPS ARE TIMELY—EARTHQUAKE IN CENTRAL ITALY

This shakemap portrays the extent of the affected areas during the devastating earthquake in central Italy during August 2016. When disaster strikes, GIS is one of the primary tools used in response and recovery. GIS practitioners and first responders map the scene, collaborate on response activities and share GIS maps broadly to support and coordinate all these efforts.

GIS MAPS FORECAST THE FUTURE — WILDFIRE SMOKE PLUMES

Smoke forecast for the next 48 hours across the continental United States in one-hour increments. In this case, the smoke forecast is shown for the Bay Area around San Francisco, Oakland and San Jose, California, alerting first responders, medical staff, and the general public to the impending health hazards.

8:00 AM

11:00 AM

1:00 PM

Smoke Forecast
63 - 158
µg/m^3

On **9/14/2016, 12:00 PM** smoke concentration levels are expected to be **63 - 158** micrograms of smoke per cubic meter of air.

Smoke levels from 89-138 µg/m^3 are unhealthy for sensitive people and levels >139 are unhealthy for all people.

Forecast created: 9/13/2016, 11:00 PM
Data updated daily

Zoom to   Get Directions

GIS MAPS CAN COMMUNICATE SCIENCE — NUCLEAR RADIATION

GIS maps are valuable tools for transparent communication. In this map, airborne radiation from the Fukushima nuclear meltdown was mapped in near real time. Unfortunately, these critical and timely maps were suppressed by the Japanese government, and initially citizens were unable to learn about areas to avoid. Scientists who shared maps like this risked their careers to communicate with the public. Ultimately, a number of senior officials lost their jobs. Timely GIS reporting helps keep governments and industry accountable. Web GIS enables map sharing with everyone.

GIS MAPS TRAVEL WITH US — AGRONOMY

GIS maps go where you go. This map of crop vitality is most useful in the field where farmers can see the information in context and take appropriate actions.

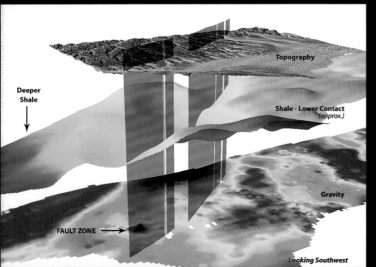

GIS MAPS SUPPORT DECISION-MAKING — OIL EXPLORATION

3D spatial analysis in GIS can support better decisions such as where to best locate your investments. In this example, you can see GIS analysis for the best place to drill for hydrocarbons in Alberta, Canada.

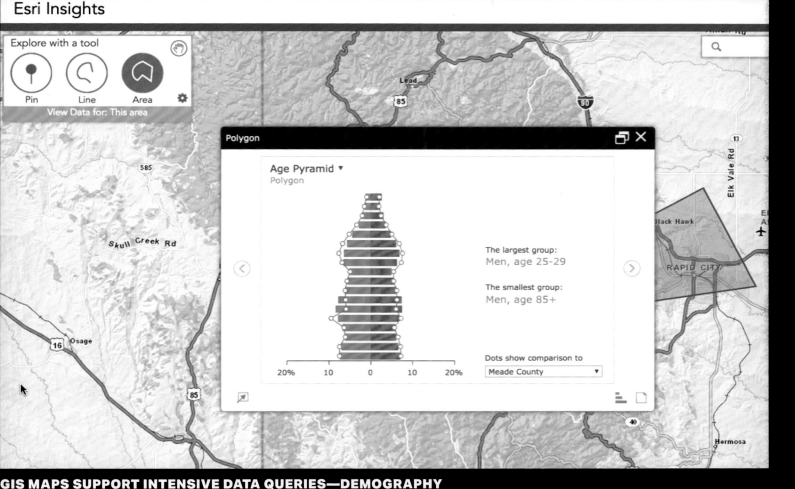

GIS MAPS SUPPORT INTENSIVE DATA QUERIES—DEMOGRAPHY

GIS maps provide windows into information sets that lie behind each map. You can retrieve a wealth of additional information by reaching through the map—such as the age by gender population statistics for Rapid City, South Dakota—by simply clicking on a feature to return deeper demographic information.

GIS IS A TOOL FOR INTEGRATION AND UNDERSTANDING

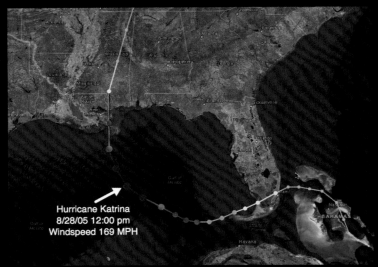

GIS MAPS CAN ANIMATE CHANGE — HURRICANE RESPONSE

In 2005 Hurricane Katrina struck New Orleans as a category 5 storm. This time series map captured the moment on August 28 when the hurricane reached maximum windspeed of 168 miles per hour just south of the Gulf Coast. Katrina continued along its path of destruction, eventually reaching into Mississippi and beyond.

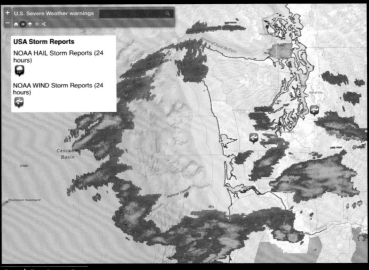

GIS MAPS SHOW STATUS — WEATHER AND STORM WARNINGS

This online map combines live feeds of severe weather data from across the United States from multiple sources, including weather radar from NEXRAD and NOAA data on temperature, wind speed and direction, precipitation, cloud cover, visibility, and real-time severe-weather warnings and advisories.

GIS MAPS ILLUMINATE SOCIAL ISSUES — THE OPIOID EPIDEMIC

Whether at the global level or the local level, social issues are driven by geography. This interactive map of opioid prescription claims (zoomed into the Eastern Seaboard of the United States) reveals the subtle geographic patterns that emerge when data is well mapped.

GIS MAPS COMMUNICATE IMPORTANCE — ZIKA

GIS maps combine data that allows us to make relative comparisons. This map of the Americas shows the areas of highest Zika virus risk in relation to the number of travelers who visit each region and who might potentially transmit the virus. For those tasked with stemming the spread of the virus, this juxtaposition puts the situation in focus.

GIS MAPS HELP MANAGE OPERATIONS IN REAL TIME — BOSTON MARATHON

GIS is used in big events such as the Boston Marathon to manage operations and communications, to ensure safety and security, and to coordinate effective response to incidents. The Operations Center for the Marathon includes a GIS dashboard with up-to-the-minute GIS maps, information feeds, and video feeds from the course.

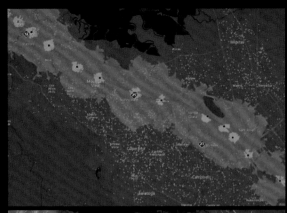

GIS MAPS CAN BE USED IN THE FIELD — UTILITY MANAGEMENT

Member of a field crew gathers information along a 430 km electric transmission line as part of an environmental study in Canada's northern wilderness. Data collection updates, as well as field communications, are transmitted to and from the enterprise GIS when workers come wthin range of suitable wireless signals.

GIS MAPS ENGAGE CITIZENS — CROWDSOURCING

Citizen reporting. Citizens in your city can report on problems and situations that they encounter daily.

GIS MAPS DRIVE EFFICIENCY — OPTIMIZING LOGISTICS AND DELIVERY

Fleets around the world apply GIS and its network optimization algorithms to make their operations more efficient (regularly cutting as much as 25 percent off their costs). Creating a delivery strategy for u rban areas requires imagination. The analysis presented here helps a multistore retail company better serve its customers by optimizing their package delivery using transit. The Station Access map (left) shows half-mile walking zones coupled with three- and five-mile travel zones for bikes and cars around transit stations. The travel map on the right shows the closest station locations for all their customers and serves as a blueprint to optimize delivery.

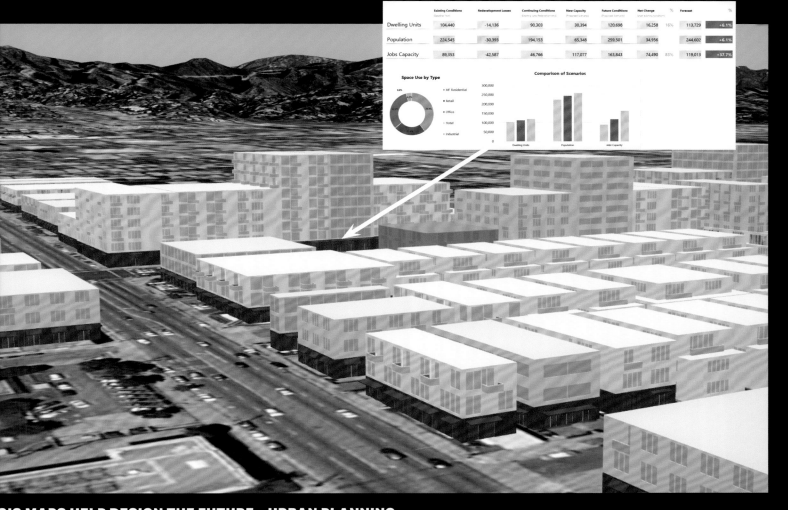

GIS MAPS HELP DESIGN THE FUTURE—URBAN PLANNING

This 3D zoning visualization of a redevelopment district in Hollywood, California helps planners evaluate and compare cityscapes that make real-world sense of the changing urban environment for residents and businesses.

BEFORE

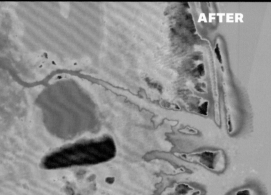

AFTER

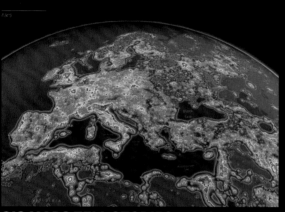

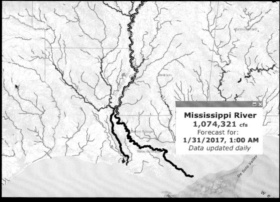

Mississippi River
1,074,321 cfs
Forecast for:
1/31/2017, 1:00 AM
Data updated daily

GIS MAPS TELL STORIES — LIGHT POLLUTION

Some 83% of the world's population–including large swaths of Europe-–cannot see the stars in the night sky. This story map reveals the best (and worst) places for amateur astronomy on the European continent and northern Africa.

GIS MODELS CAN FORECAST RIVER FLOW AND FLOODING — HYDROLOGY

This map is a forecast model that predicts the flow for over 2.7 million river reaches for the entire United States. It takes the precipitation forecast from the National Weather Service and mathematically computes physical processes such as snowmelt, infiltration, and the movement of water across the terrain. This short-term forecast is computed every hour for the next 15 hours at one-hour intervals. These maps are updated hourly This is big data and big computing.

GIS MAPS ARE USED FOR QUANTITAIVE ANALYSIS — DAMAGE ASSESSMENT

After Hurricane Irene struck the Outer Banks of North Carolina in 2011, local highway officials used GIS analysis of lidar data to measure the extent to which the sea encroached on the community (and the amount of sand it took with it on the way out). So accurate were the measurements that officials were able to calculate how many dump truckloads of sand would be required to breach the gap and begin rebuilding the primary roadway that had been washed away.

MAKING SENSE OF A FRAGILE RESOURCE—MARINE ECOLOGY

A deeper understanding of marine ecosystems is now accessible from an online app. Although 95% of the ocean still remains a mystery, we depend on it for survival. This is a map of Ecological Marine Units (EMUs), which are 3D, data-driven, physically distinct regions from the surface down to the ocean floor. The EMU Explorer allows you to better understand the ocean conditions anywhere on Earth, including off the coast of Kauai in the state of Hawaii.

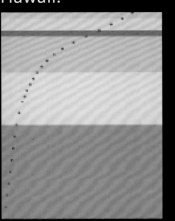

TEMPERATURE

MAPS ARE APPS

Every GIS map has an interface - a user experience for putting that map to use. These experiences are called "apps," and they bring GIS to life for all kinds of people. And as with other apps, these maps work virtually everywhere: on your mobile phones, tablets, in web browsers, and on desktops. GIS apps enable all kinds of people to tap into the power of GIS to understand and take action.

PLANNERS USE GIS APPS TO ANALYZE CRITICAL QUESTIONS

Analytical insight is critical to deeply understand the implications of alternate planning scenarios. In this example, a city analyst uses the GeoPlanner app to combine map overlays and test various scenarios.

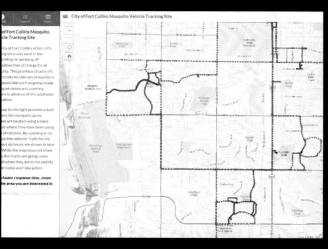

BROWSER-BASED APPS FACILITATE COMMUNICATION

The city of Fort Collins, Colorado, keeps its citizens informed about mosquito abatement operations in real time on the web.

FIELD WORKFORS COORDINATION AND NAVIGATION

GIS is used in thousands of organizations to coordinate work in their offices and in the field. GIS maps can go anywhere, with or without a wireless signal, connecting staff with their work and providing a platform for coordination and collaboration across teams.

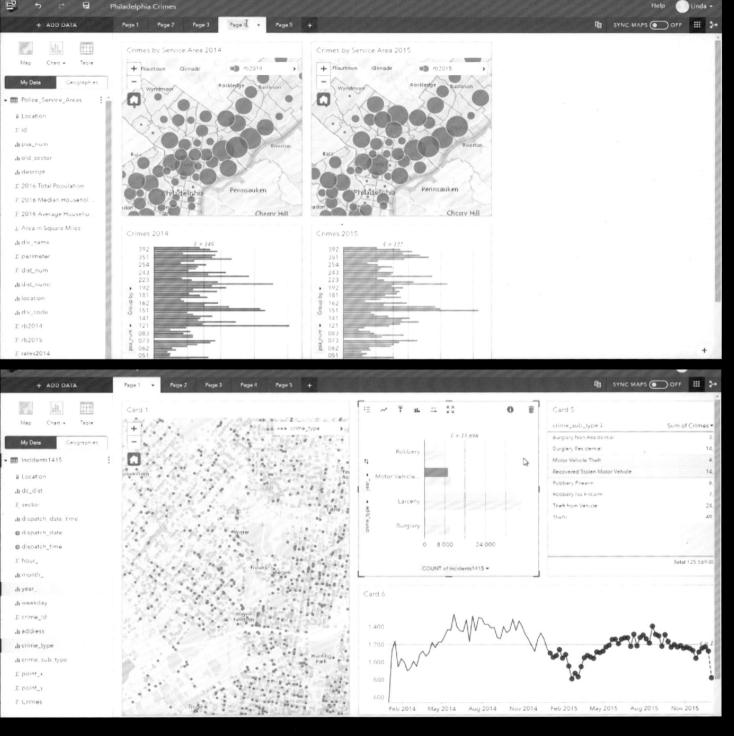

INSIGHTS APP FOR EXPLORING YOUR MAPS AND DATA

People everywhere use the Insights app to explore and interpret GIS data layers using maps and charts. You can integrate additional rich layers to help you investigate your data more deeply while discovering new patterns.

GIS IS MOBILE

GIS on mobile devices is changing how we interact with geography. With your phone, you can access GIS maps and data anywhere, positioning you and your organization to leverage full GIS capabilities in the field. A GIS-enabled smartphone is also an advanced live data sensor.

3D GIS APPS ON YOUR TABLET

3D GIS can guide you with alerts and routes for emergencies.

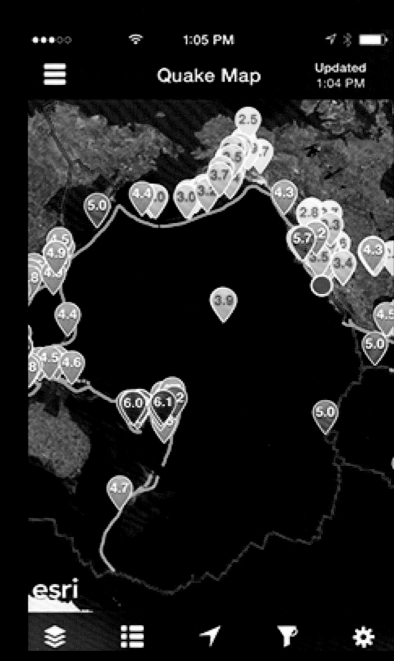

PROVIDING GEO-ALERTS

Mobile apps can alert you to events on the basis of your location. The quake feed app uses your location to send you alerts about earthquakes near you.

GIS IN THE SKY

Professional-quality imagery and 3D data can be generated from drone-captured images and put this high-resolution data to work for GIS visualization and analysis. The workflow is surprisingly simple: 1 Fly the mission (the blue dots are capture points), 2 Capture oblique views (4 of 24 are shown above), 3 Create the 3D scene (in under 30 minutes after downloading images off the drone).

GIS MAPS LET YOU ORBIT THE EARTH

This application maps the current location of about 14,000 man-made objects orbiting Earth. The data is maintained by Space-Track.org, an organization that promotes space flight safety, protection of the space environment, and the peaceful use of space by sharing situational awareness information with US and international satellite operators and other entities.

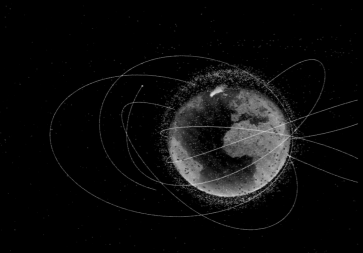

APPLYING 3D ANYWHERE

This regional 3D scene presents surfaces of interesting places on our planet, featuring World Imagery along with Terrain layers. You can click on the slides in the scene to explore them and navigate within each location to see different perspectives for each place.

BUILDINGS AND INTERIORS

GIS doesn't stop at the building level. Indoor mapping and routing of campuses and other office environments is rapidly gaining traction in the facilities management world.

A VIRTUAL TOUR OF VENICE ITALY

3D City Model of Venice, Italy. This view of Venice's famous landmarks in Saint Mark's Square—Saint Mark's Cathedral, the Doge's Palace, and the Campanile Bell Tower—along with geo-typical building models for the rest of the city, created using ArcGIS Pro.

BIG DATA AND CLIMATE MODELING

Time series and temporal maps create an opportunity to systematically make comparisons over time.

PROJECTING FUTURE CLIMATE CONDITIONS

The Community Climate System Model (CCSM) provides projections for future climate conditions. The model is run under a variety of future scenarios. Model outputs span the globe, providing monthly projections over the next century for precipitation, temperature, and other global factors. The results forecast the future change in climate throughout the 21st century.

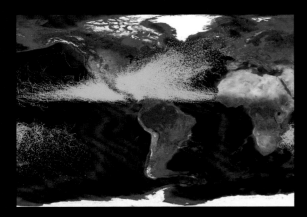

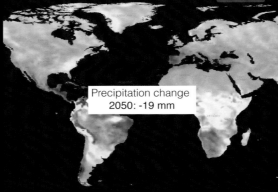

Precipitation change
2050: -19 mm

Temperature change
2050: + 2.1 Celsius

HISTORICAL HURRICANE

Hurricanes carve a well-worn belt right around the planet—a storm band in the Northern Hemisphere and another in the Southern Hemisphere. This map records the locations and storm paths of every hurricane and tropical storm since the mid-1800s.

PRECIPITATION PROJECTION FOR 2050

Model estimate for projected changes in precipitation for a single month in the year 2050. This is but one of the monthly maps that are computed for every month and year for 100 years. Maps like these are often animated, much like the weather maps on your nightly news.

TEMPERATURE PROJECTION FOR 2050

A snapshot in time for projected changes in temperature for the same month in the year 2050.

BIG DATA AND THE INTERNET OF THINGS (IoT)

GIS and geography provide a spatial framework to organize and work with big data and sensor feeds in a variety of forms. Analyzing and seeing this big data in a geographic context reveals deep insights that lead to understanding and action. In fact, a geospatialframework is required to work effectively with sensors and big data sources.

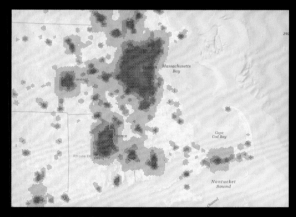

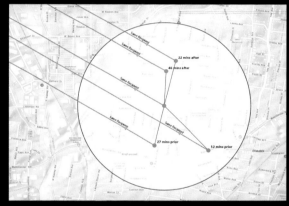

HEAT MAP OF DAILY FINANCIAL TRANSACTIONS

Billions of financial transfers are made daily. With so much money moving through these systems electronically, the need to flush fraudulent activity out of a flood of activity is critical. GIS provides an effective tool for discovering fraud. This map shows the frequency and mass of each day's financial transactions along the Eastern Seaboard of the United States.

SUSPICIOUS TRANSACTIONS

Mining suspicious observations from billions of financial transactions. A subset of transactions is identified that included the same destination, within a small time window and from locations within a close proximity of one another.

TRANSACTION ORIGINS AND DESTINATIONS

ANALYSIS

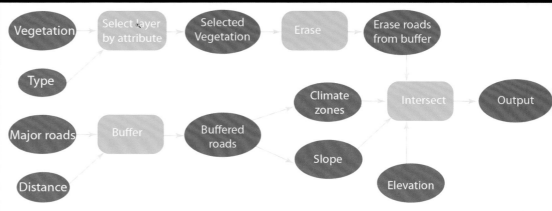

COUGAR SUSTAINABILITY ANALYSIS

This shows how GIS was used to model cougar habitat in the mountains and wildlands near Los Angeles. Wildlife conservation experts stress the need to identify safe corridors, including habitat bridges, so the big cats in isolated populations can find each other.

ROOFTOP SOLAR POTENTIAL

The state of Minnesota modeled solar potential for the whole state by deriving solar radiation and aspect from elevation, vegetation, and other critical raster and imagery layers. This enables citizens to perform a quick, high-level assessment of where solar power might be a practical alternative for their locations.

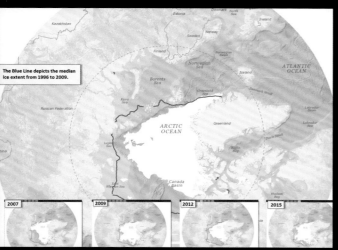

FINDING PATTERNS - POLAR ICE EXTENT

Ice in the polar regions is in a continuous state of flux. No one denies that the ice extent and thickness are on the wane. Huge volumes of imagery and datasets are being collected and assembled into a valuable research tool for increasing our understanding of the massive changes that are under way at our poles.

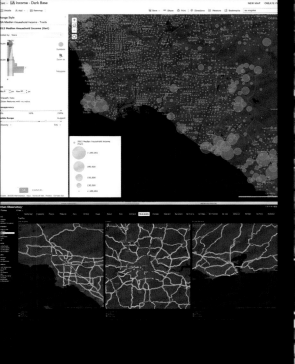

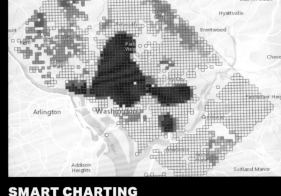

SMART MAPPING

Smart mapping is a new way of creating maps online. Using intelligent defaults, data-driven workflows, and an interactive user interface that invites data exploration, you can easily uncover additional details about your data that were hidden from view.

SMART CHARTING

Finding the signal in the noise. Visualizing maps side-by-side with charts helps uncover patterns, trends, relationships, and structure in data that may otherwise be difficult to see. In this data display we see the spatial distribution of total crime incidents in Washington, DC in the heat map while statistics charted by time of day and type of crime reveal a different perspectuve couldn't be discerned from mapping only locations.

Alaska Ice:
Documenting Glaciers on the Move

Retreating: Muir Glacier

Muir Glacier ×

Earthstar Geographics, CNES/Airbus DS

GLACIAL RETREAT OVER TIME
This story map offers convincing evidence about a warming Alaska. The range of shared imagery and GIS applications by many in the GIS community is profound.

CROWDSOURCING NATIONAL PARKS

In celebration of the 100th anniversary of the National Park Service, the agency released an innovative Story Map application that allows the public to share their favorite photos and experiences in America's national parks. The ever-changing story is intimate and fascinating.

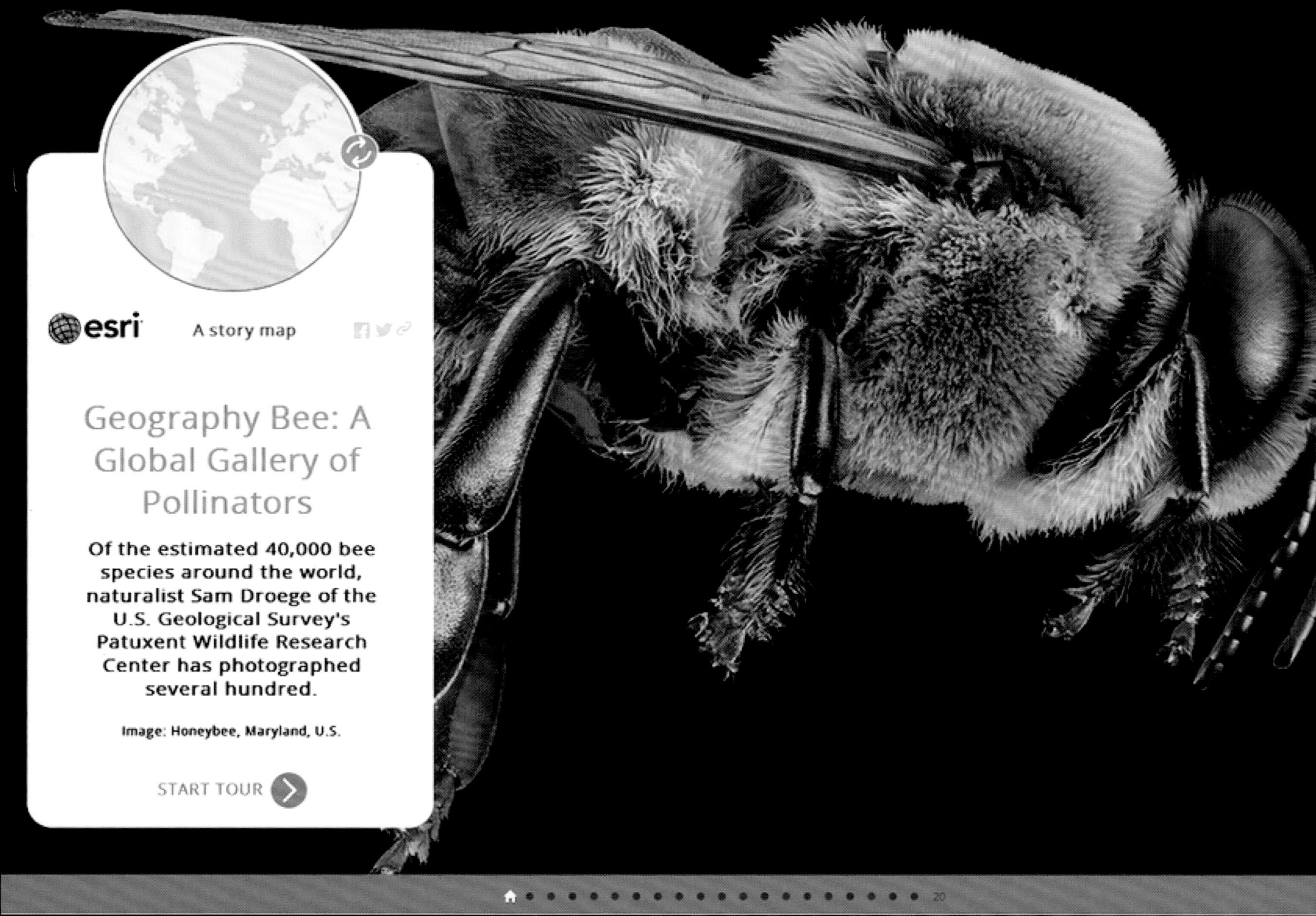

esri · A story map

Geography Bee: A Global Gallery of Pollinators

Of the estimated 40,000 bee species around the world, naturalist Sam Droege of the U.S. Geological Survey's Patuxent Wildlife Research Center has photographed several hundred.

Image: Honeybee, Maryland, U.S.

START TOUR

20

SPECIES OVERVIEW
Geography Bee features exquisite insect photography coupled with global species location overviews.

Alan Lomax's Online Archive at the Association for Cultural Equity

Boyd Rivers and Ruth May

"Come Out the Wildnerness," performed by Boyd Rivers and his wife Ruth May. Preceded by introduction of themselves and their music. Shot by Alan Lomax, John Bishop, and Worth Long, August 30, 1978, at the Rivers' home in Canton, Mississippi.

Boyd Rivers & Ruth May Rivers: Come Ou...

On the Greenville Levee (1978)

In the summer of 1978, Alan Lomax, John Bishop, and Worth Long spent two days on the levee in Greenville, Mississippi, interviewing

107

STORIES OF MUSICAL HERITAGE

Alan Lomax was an American field collector of folk music of the 20th century. This story map links his online video and audio archive recently released by the Association of Cultural Equity along with their map locations, revealing the fascinating link between geography and the origins of American music.

ESRI USER CONFERENCE POSTERS
Posters from succesive Esri User Conferences, using the mottos *Understanding Precedes Action, You Only Understand Something Relative to Something You Already Understand* and *Transforming Big Data Into Big*

Understanding Precedes Action.™

Richard Saul Wurman
Jon Kamen
Jack Dangermond

ESRI User Conference
July 2010
San Diego, California

192021 is a multi-media initiative that will reveal unique patterns in urbanization and make comparative data accessible and relevant to the general public, government agencies, academic institutions, organizations and business leaders.

This groundbreaking partnership between **Richard Saul Wurman, ESRI,** and **@radical.media** is seeking to build a valuable resource to help us understand all aspects of urban life in the 21st century.

192021

192021

WWW.192021.ORG

DESIGN BY: @radical.media

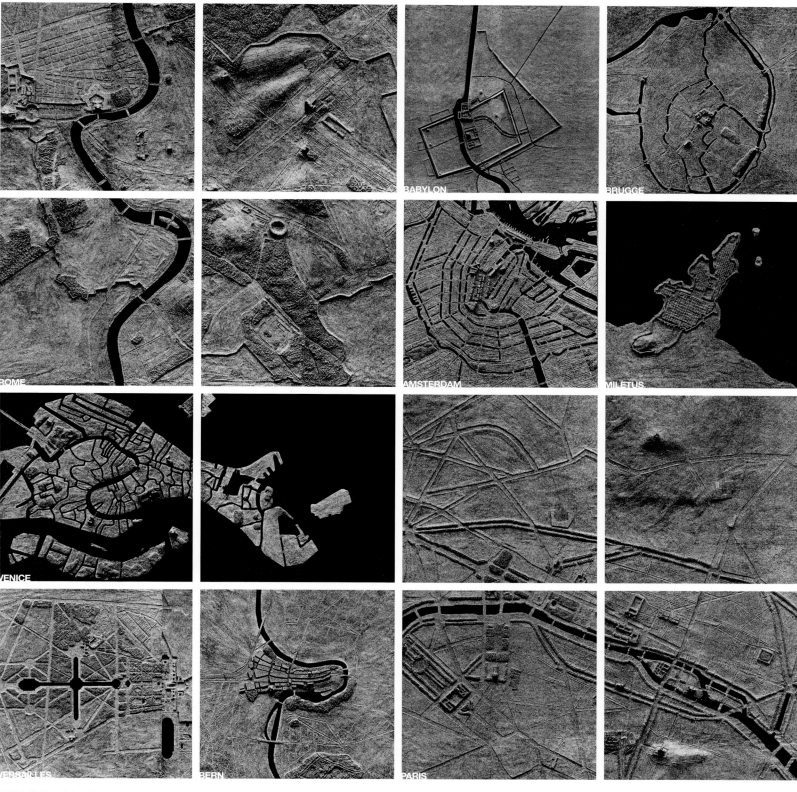

BABYLON

BRUGGE

ROME

AMSTERDAM

MILETUS

109

VENICE

VERSAILLES

BERN

PARIS

In 1962 Richard Saul Wurman developed his first law of understanding: You only understand something relative to something you understand.

This took the physical form of a small publication of diagrammatic 3D maps of 50 ancient, contemporary and proposed cities. Displaying only gross form characteristics such as roads, major bodies of water, wooded areas and building complexes. The critical decision was to create them using the same scale and display techniques.

This and later laws led to the 'urban atlas' of 1967, which clarified the statistical grammar of magnitude. As a result, Wurman coined, in 1975, the name 'information architecture' for that new field of work.

112121 is a multi-media initiative that will reveal unique patterns in urbanization and make comparative data accessible and relevant to the general public, government agencies, academic institutions, organizations and business leaders.

This groundbreaking partnership between Richard Saul Wurman, ESRI, and @radical.media is seeking to build a valuable resource to help us understand all aspects of urban life in the 21st century.

192021 Understanding Precedes Action.

"You only understand something relative to something you already understand."

Urban Observatory™

A 192021 Project

192021 is a multi-media initiative that will reveal unique patterns in urbanization and make comparative data accessible and relevant to the general public, government agencies, academic institutions, organizations and business leaders.

This groundbreaking partnership between Richard Saul Wurman, ESRI, and @radical.media is seeking to build a valuable resource to help us understand all aspects of urban life in the 21st century.

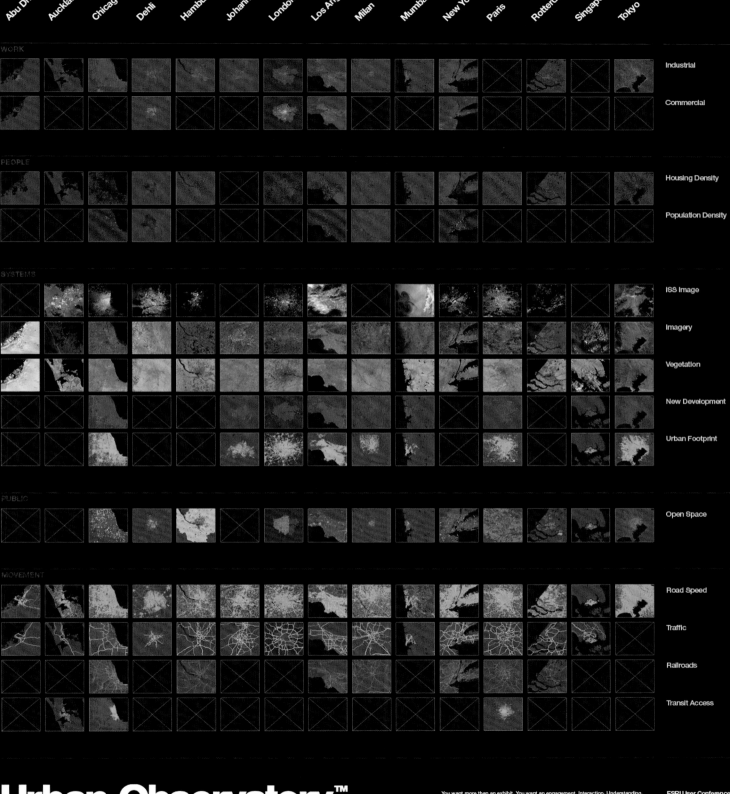

Abu Dhabi · Auckland · Chicago · Dehli · Hamburg · Johannesburg · London · Los Angeles · Milan · Mumbai · New York City · Paris · Rotterdam · Singapore · Tokyo

WORK
- Industrial
- Commercial

PEOPLE
- Housing Density
- Population Density

SYSTEMS
- ISS Image
- Imagery
- Vegetation
- New Development
- Urban Footprint

PUBLIC
- Open Space

MOVEMENT
- Road Speed
- Traffic
- Railroads
- Transit Access

Urban Observatory™

You want more than an exhibit. You want an engagement. Interaction. Understanding.
Richard Saul Wurman, @Radical.Media, and ESRI bring you the Urban Observatory.

Experience simultaneous views of dynamic, flowing content about work, people, places, movement, and systems. Look at questions and answers impacting today's global cities. You will be able to compare and contrast complex systems using visualized information for a clearer understanding of life in the 21st century.

ESRI User Conference 2013

Transforming
Big Data Into
Big Understanding.

Urban Observatory™
19 20 21 Project

2014

**ESRI
International
User
Conference**

San Diego, CA

2015

**The
Smithsonian
Institute**

Washington DC

19 20 21 is a multi-media initiative that will reveal unique patterns in urbanization and make comparative data accessible and relevant to the general public, government agencies, academic institutions, organizations and business leaders.

This groundbreaking partnership between **Richard Saul Wurman, ESRI,** and **RadicalMedia™** is seeking to establish methodologies and resources to help us understand all aspects of urban life in the 21st century.

POSTER DESIGN:
FREDERIC SIMON

MAP DATA:
ESRI

WWW.192021.ORG
WWW.URBANOBSERVATORY.ORG

19 20 21

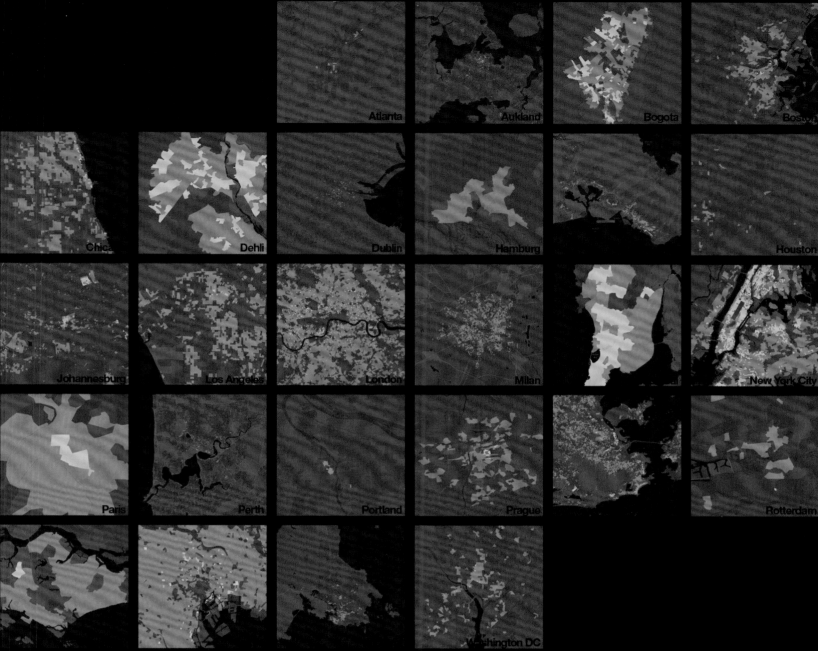

Urban Observatory™

Cities do not collect, transcribe, or notate their data at the same scale, with the same symbols, colors, or legends. The result is that cities do not speak the same language.

A map is a pattern made understandable. You must be able to compare patterns in order to fully understand cities' successes, failures, and opportunities.

Urban Observatory™ demonstrates this new paradigm by creating comparative cartography and a single language.

Urban Observatory™ is an interactive exhibit that enables you to compare and contrast data from cities around the world.

A 192021 project currently in development by Richard Saul Wurman, RadicalMedia, and ESRI, that aims to make the world's data both understandable and useful.

ESRI
International
User
Conference

Cities

Abu Dhabi
Accra
Albuquerque
Algiers
Anaheim
Anchorage
Arlington VA
Arlington TX
Atlanta
Auckland
Aurora
Austin
Bakersfield
Baltimore
Bangkok
Baton Rouge
Beijing
Berlin
Birmingham
Bogota
Boise
Boston
Bristol
Buenos Aires
Buffalo
Cairo
Cardiff
Chandler
Charlotte
Chesapeake
Chicago
Chula Vista
Cincinnati
Cleveland
Colorado Springs
Columbus
Corpus Christi
Dallas
Delhi
Denver
Detroit
Dublin
Dubuque
Durham
Edinburgh
Ekurhuleni
El Paso
Fargo

Fort Wayne
Fort Worth
Fremont
Fresno
Garland
Gavie
Geneva
Glasgow
Glendale
Greensboro
Hamburg
Henderson
Hialeah
Honolulu
Houston
Indianpolis
Irvine
Irving
Iskandar Malaysia
Istanbul
Jacksonville
Jeddah
Jersey City
Johannesburg
Kansas City
Kolkata
Kuwait City
Lagos
Las Vegas
Leeds
Lexington
Lincoln
Liverpool
London
Long Beach
Los Angeles
Louisville
Lubbock
Madison
Madrid
Manchester
Manila
Medellin
Memphis
Mesa
Mexico City
Miami
Milan
Milwaukee
Minneapolis
Montgomery
Moscow
Mumbai
Nairobi
Nashville
New Orleans

Newark
Norfolk
Las Vegas
Oakland
Oklahoma City
Omaha
Orlando
Paris
Perth
Peterborough
Philadelphia
Phoenix
Pittsburgh
Plano
Portland
Prague
Raleigh
Reno
Richmond
Rio de Janeiro
Riverside
Rotterdam
Sacramento
San Antonio
San Diego
San Francisco
San Jose
Santa Ana
Santiago
Sao Paulo
Scottsdale
Seattle
Sevilla
Shanghai
Singapore
Sioux Falls
St Louis
St Paul
St Petersburg
Stockton
Swansea
Sydney
Tampa
Teheran
Tokyo
Toledo
Tshwane
Tucson
Tulsa
Victoria
Virginia Beach
Washington, D.C.
Wichita
Winston-Salem
Yakima

Themes

Work

Commercial
Industrial
Dominant Occupations

Movement

Highway Access
Roadspeed
Traffic
Railroads
Transit Access
Airports
Ports

People

Housing Density
Population Density
Senior Population
Youth Population

Public

Open Space
ParkScore
Health Resources

Systems

Current Temperatures
From the ISS
Imagery
Urban Footprint
Winds
Historical Boundaries
Flood Zones
Impaired Water
New Development

Urban Observatory

CHAPTER CREDIT

Jim Herries
Hugh Keegan

The Urban Observatory provides a comparative understanding of our world. It tells the story of the global community through analysis of our largest, most unique urban cities. Users compare facts and live data about multiple cities through the use of interactive maps and standardized sets of information in a side-by-side layout of maps for comparing places.

The Urban Observatory is both a visual representation of questions and answers that lead to understanding as well as a recognition and celebration of humans and their capacity to create. Perhaps equally important, it demonstrates the power of geography and maps as a common language for understanding.

Why is the Urban Observatory so powerful? What makes the Urban Observatory so valuable is that the data can be visualized and contextualized for comparative analysis. Government agencies at all levels, private businesses, nonprofit organizations, and individual citizens can all benefit by accessing rich, live content that's continuously updated.

Specific data indicators provide information about people, their use of the land, and the infrastructure needed to service those uses. Each map provides an easy-to-understand view of a city. They cross-cut areas for both Urban Observatory participation and experience.

The world's largest and most influential cities are joining this first-of-its-kind information experience and user architecture that takes advantage of GIS as an integration and communication platform. By contributing, these cities empower citizens, constituents, colleagues, and the global community.

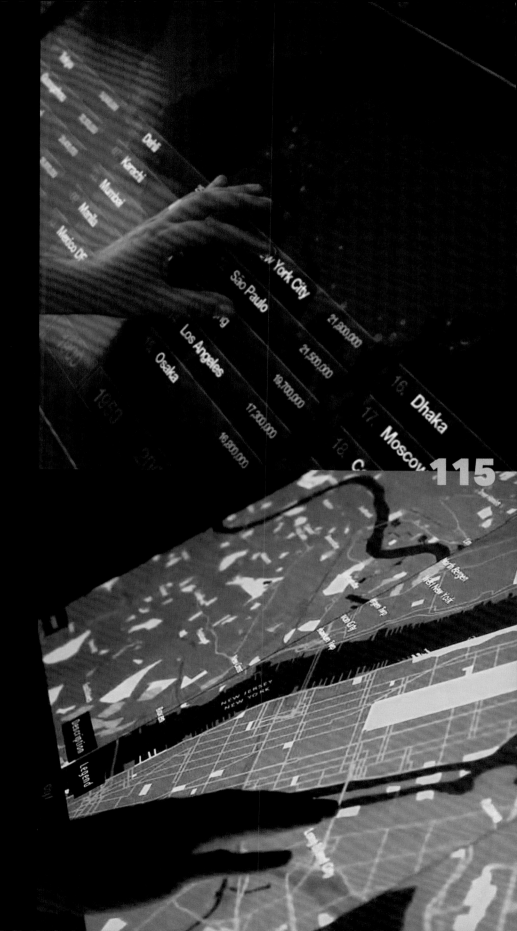

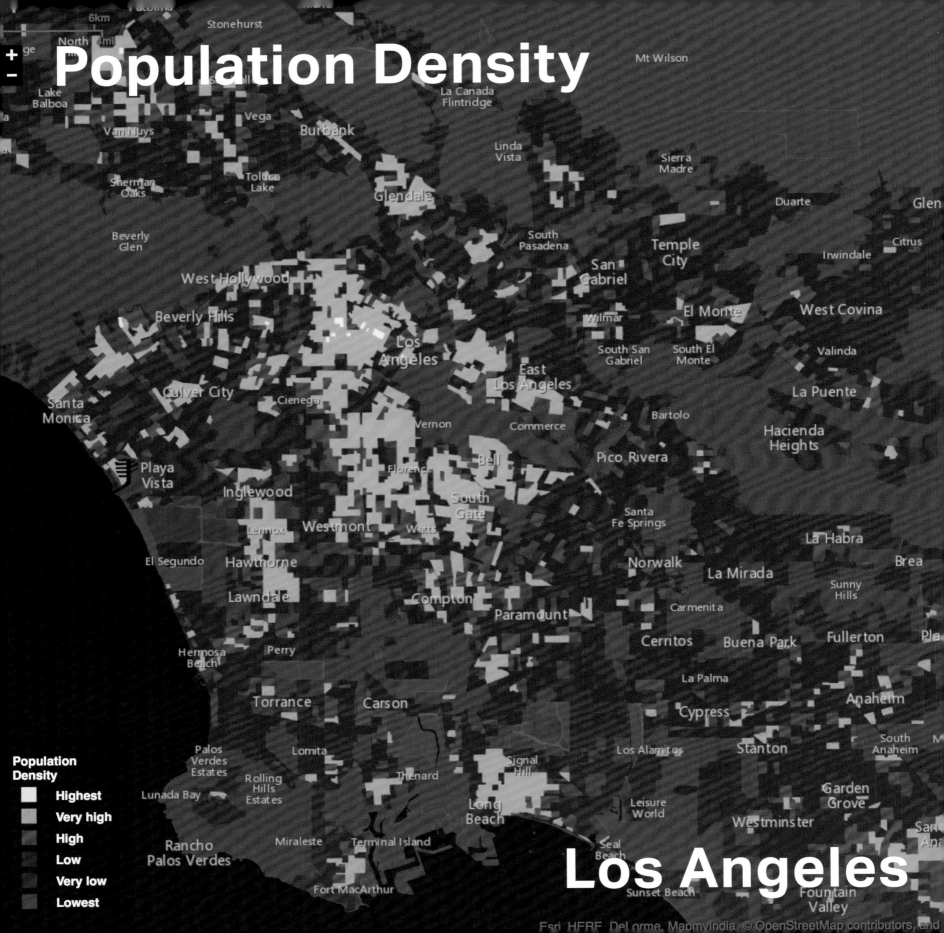

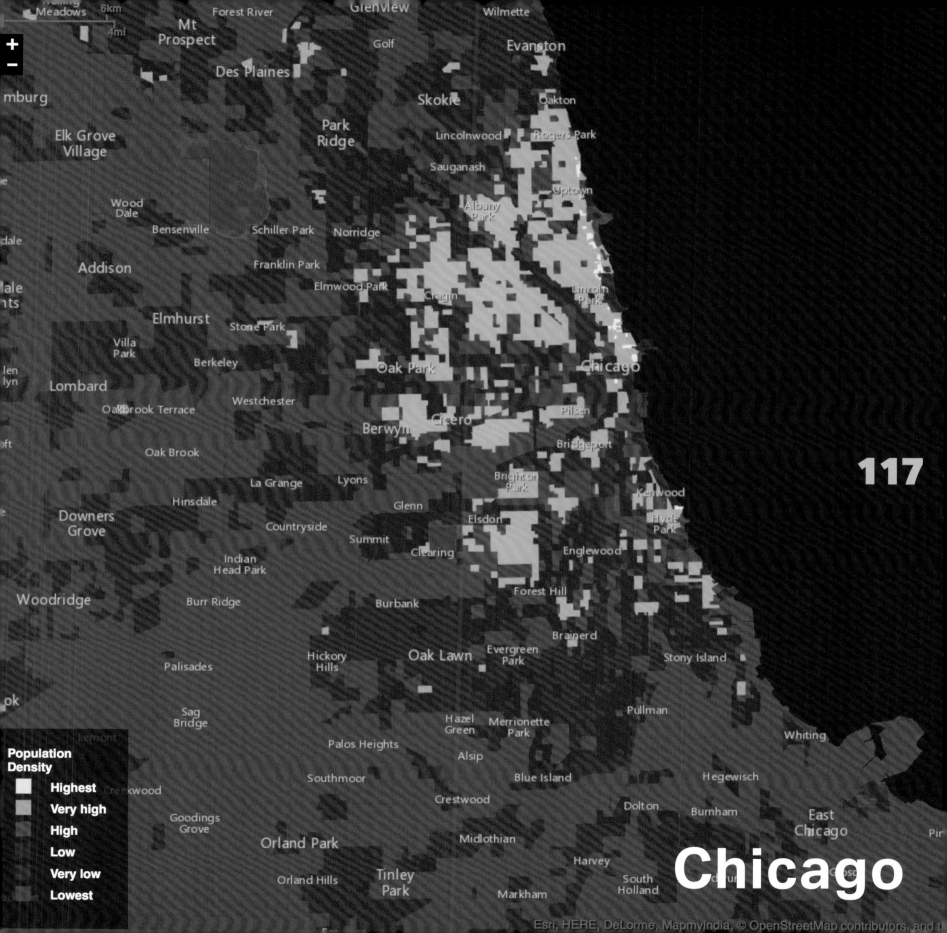

117

Chicago

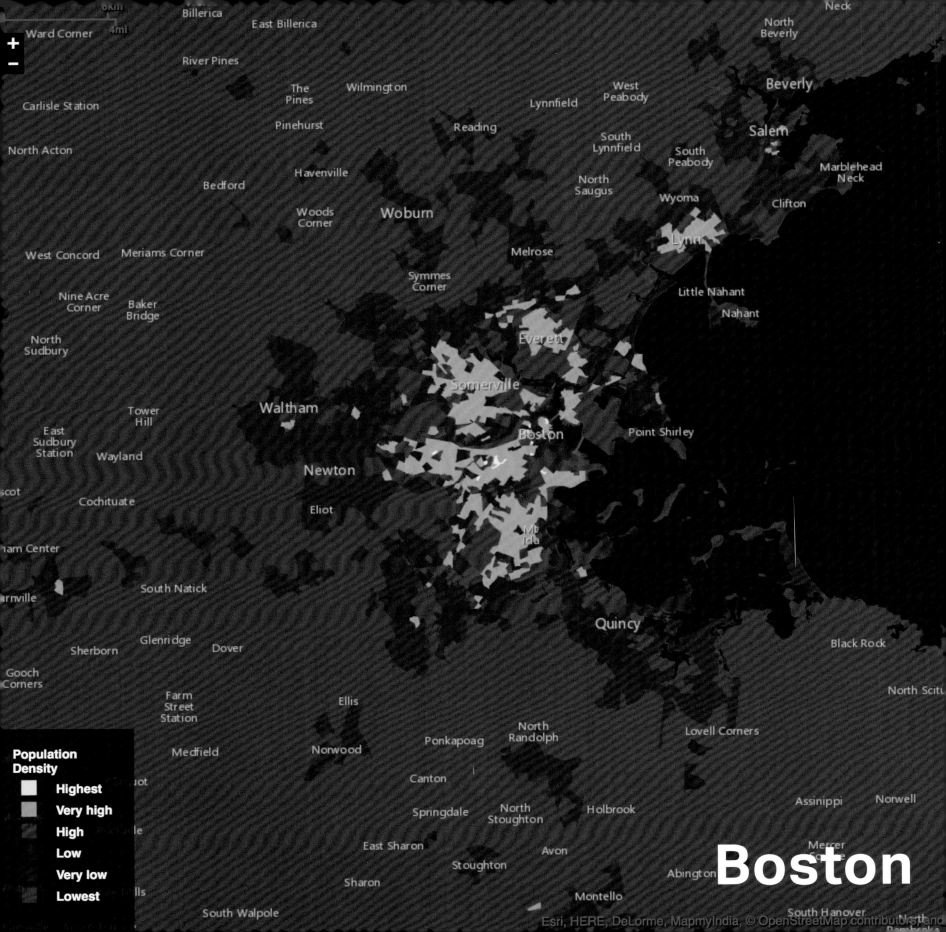

Boston

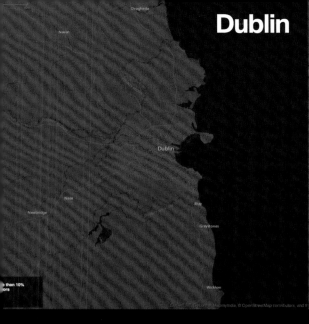
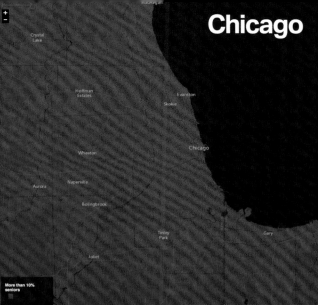
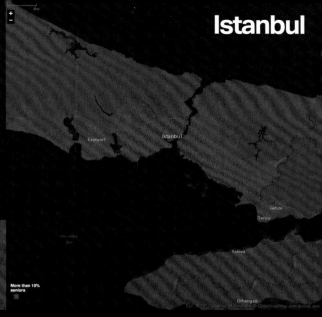

Senior Population

This map shows where seniors reside in the city, and emphasizes areas where seniors are more than 10% of the total. The map layers show a dot distribution to represent the population, where each dot represents a number of people age 65 and over in that area.

The dot values are adjusted by scale to get the best representation of the distribution. The value of each dot is roughly halved with each increase in scale, from 100 persons per dot at city-wide scales, to 3 persons per dot at neighborhood scale. For areas which contain a high proportion

of seniors (more than 10%), added emphasis is given a transparent polygon underneath the dots.

Youth Population

This map shows where youth reside in the city, and emphasizes areas where youth are more than 33% of the total population. The map layers show a dot distribution to represent the population, where each dot represents a number of people age 18 or below

in that area. The dot values are adjusted by scale to get the best representation of the distribution. The value of each dot is roughly halved with each increase in scale, from 100 persons per dot at city- wide scales, to 3 persons per dot at neighborhood scale. For areas which contain

a high proportion of youth (more than 33%), added emphasis is given a transparent polygon underneath the dots.

119

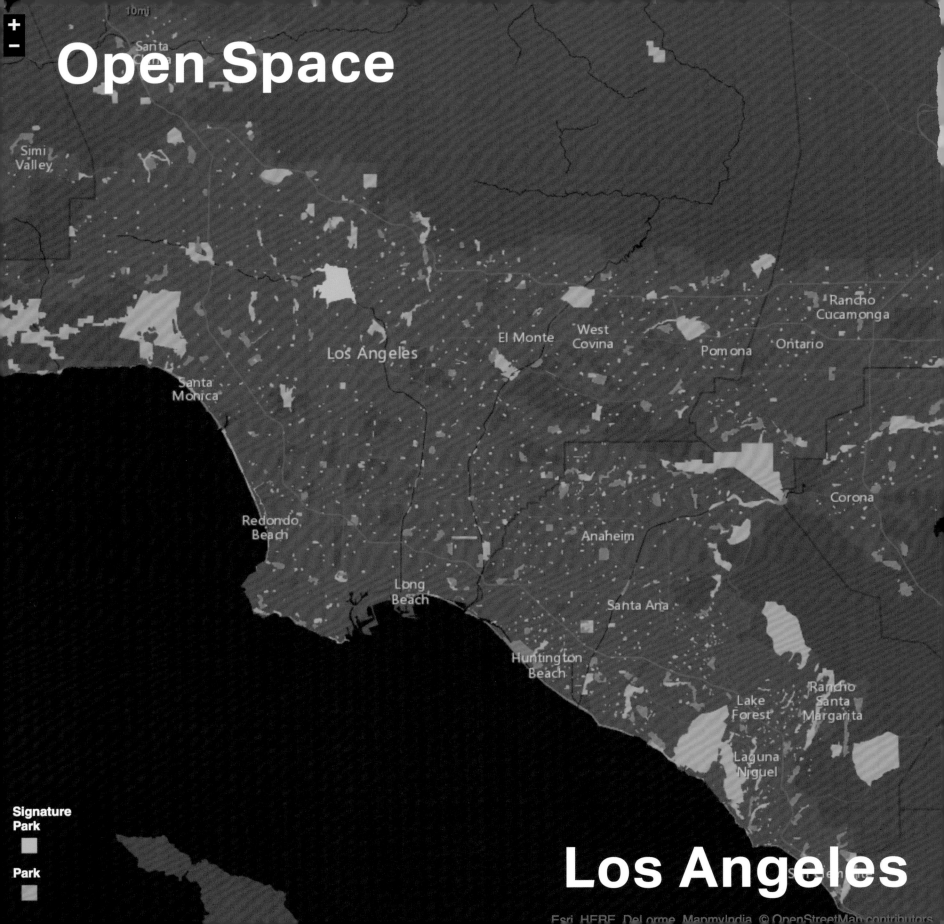

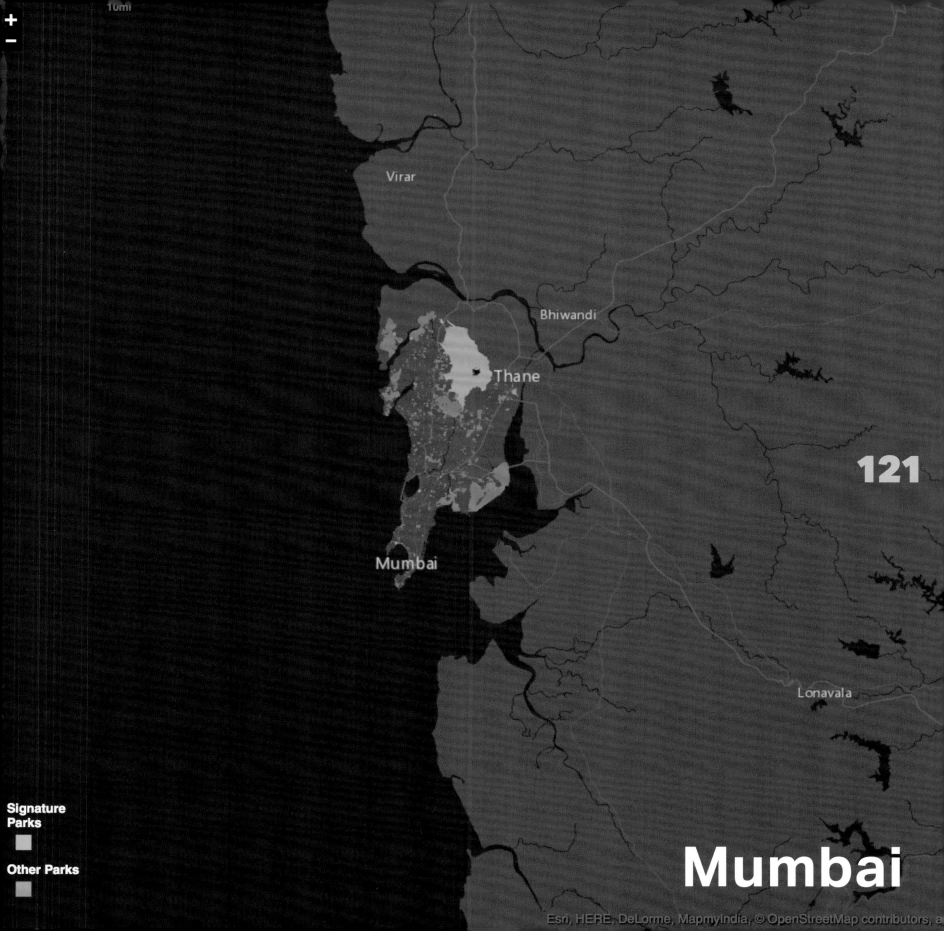

121

Mumbai

Signature
Parks

Other Parks

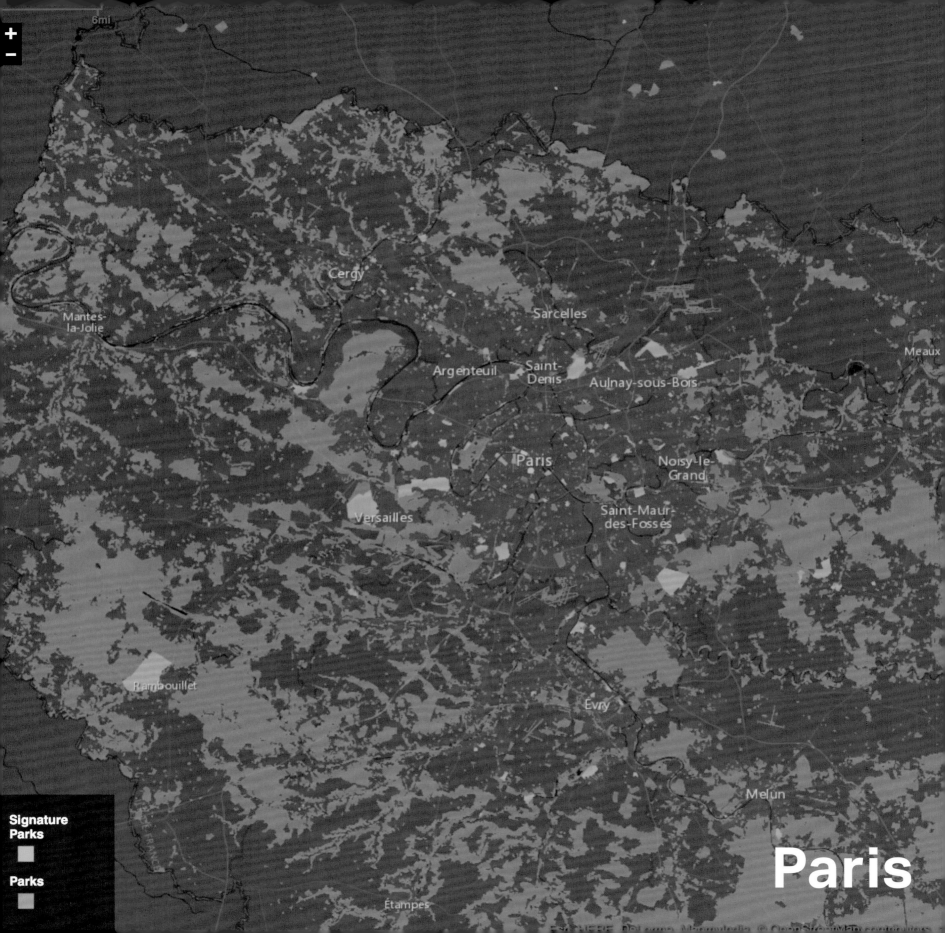

Paris

Industrial

This map shows areas dedicated to industrial landuse.

Commercial

This map shows areas dedicated to commercial landuse.

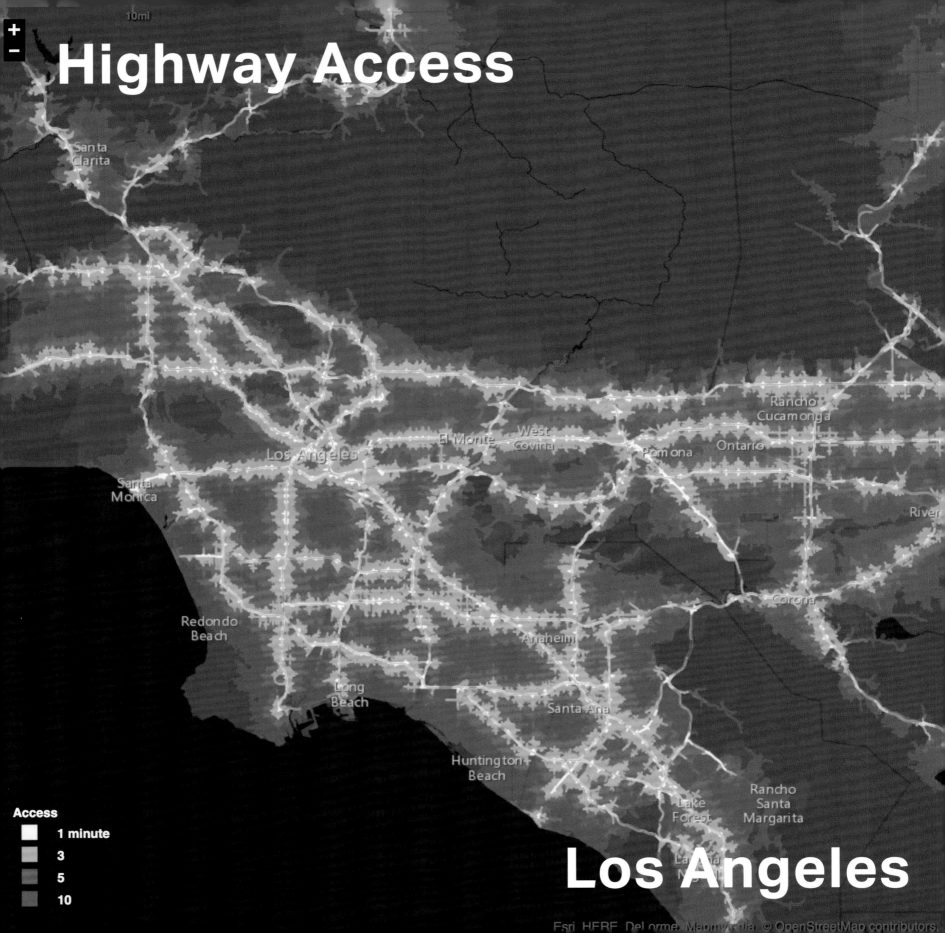

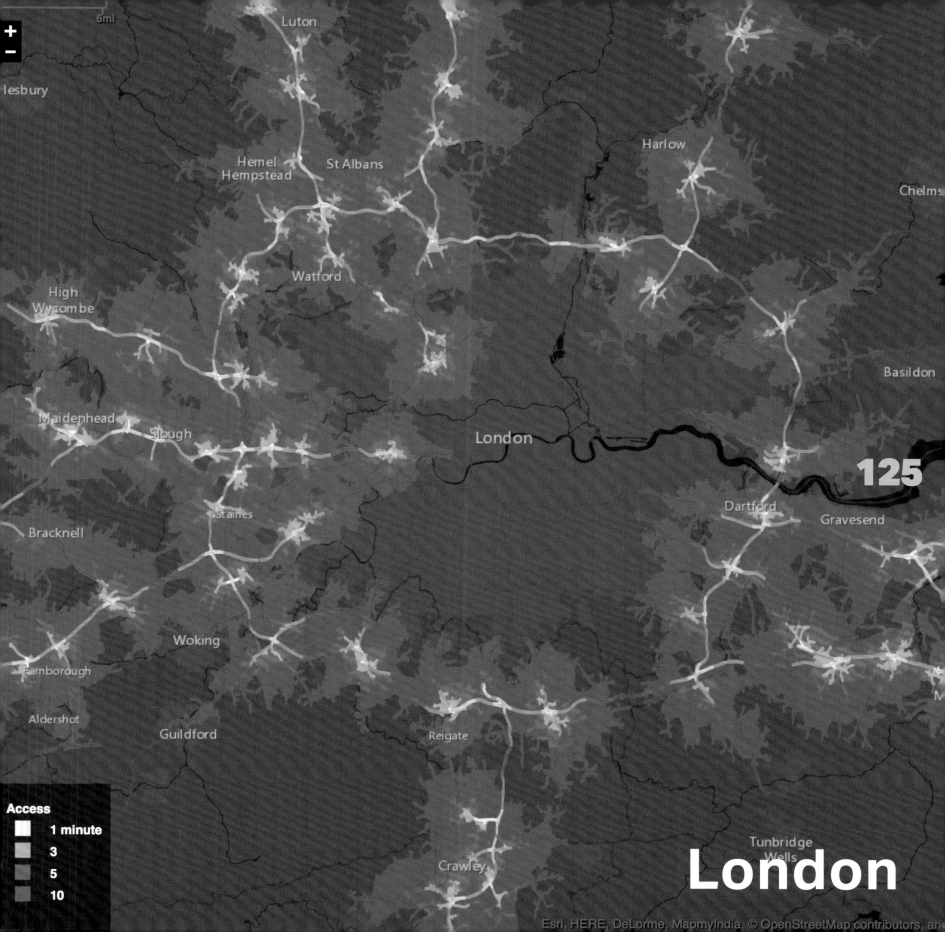

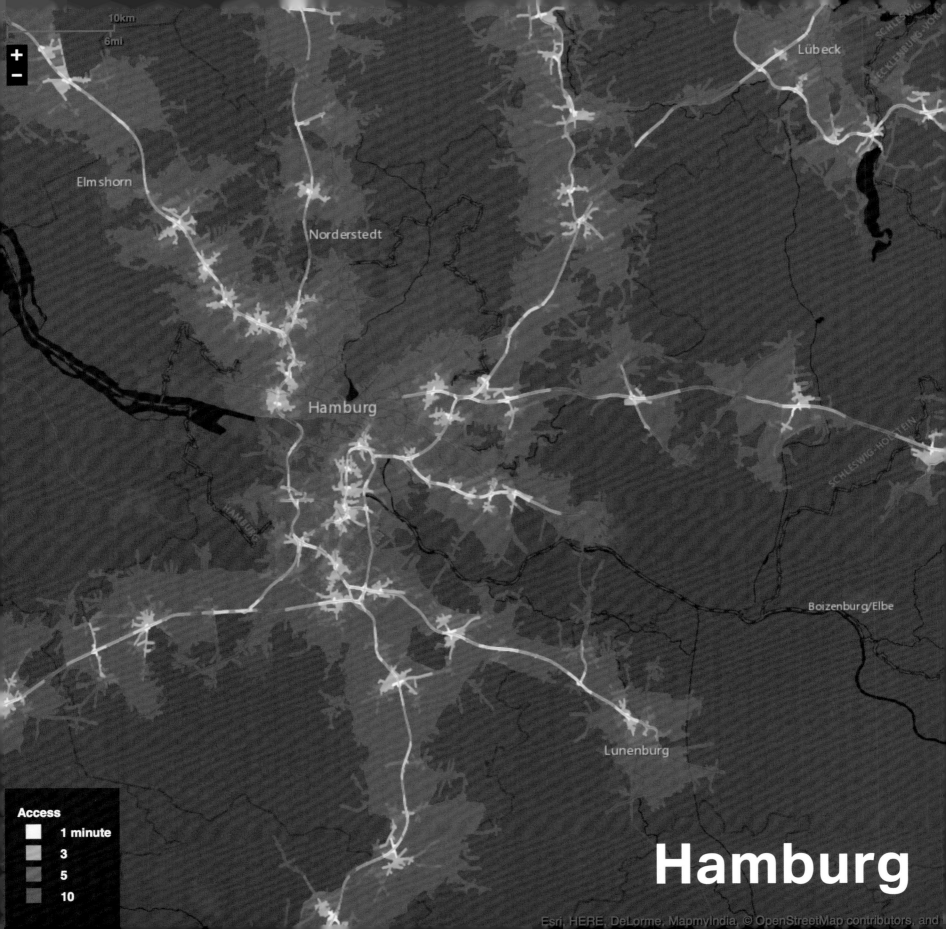

Hamburg

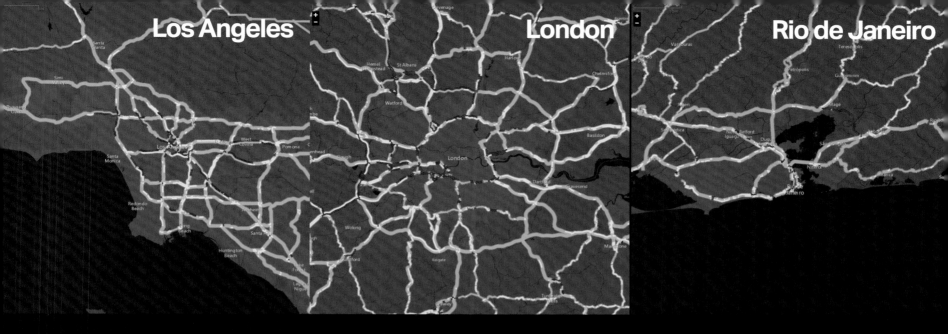

Traffic

This map shows the traffic conditions you can expect at a certain time of day in this city.

Railroads

This map shows railroads in and around the city.

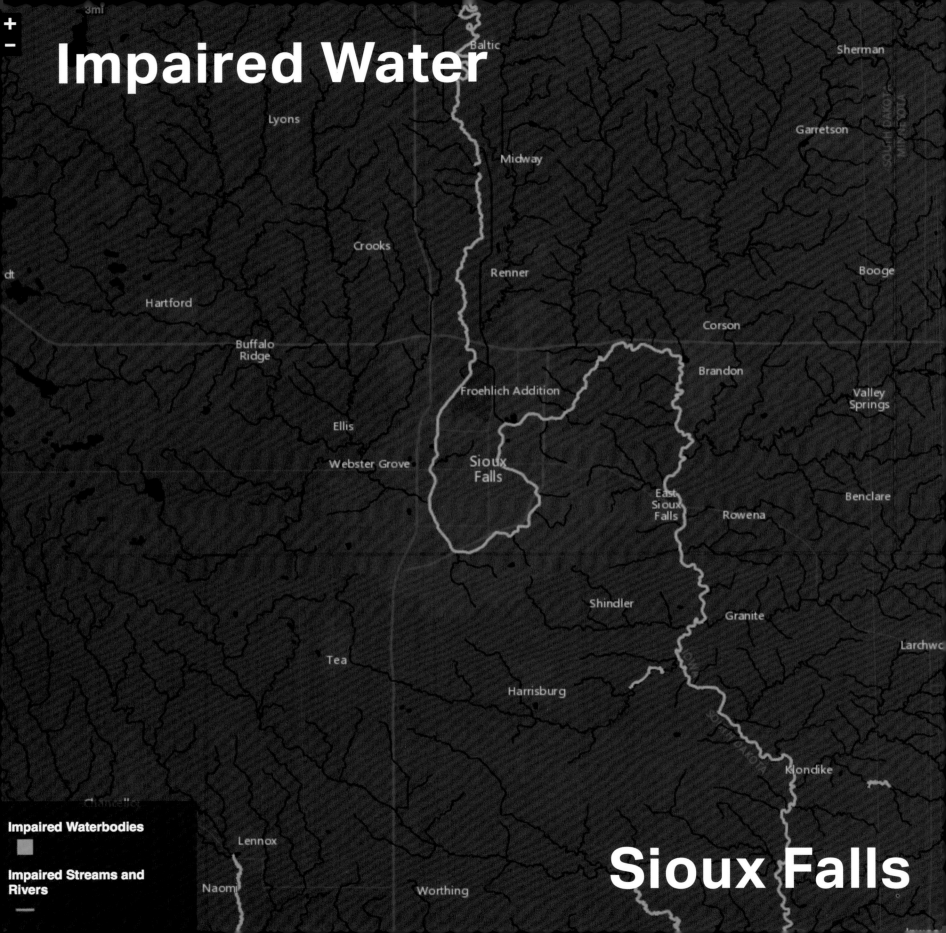

Impaired Waterbodies

Impaired Streams and
Rivers

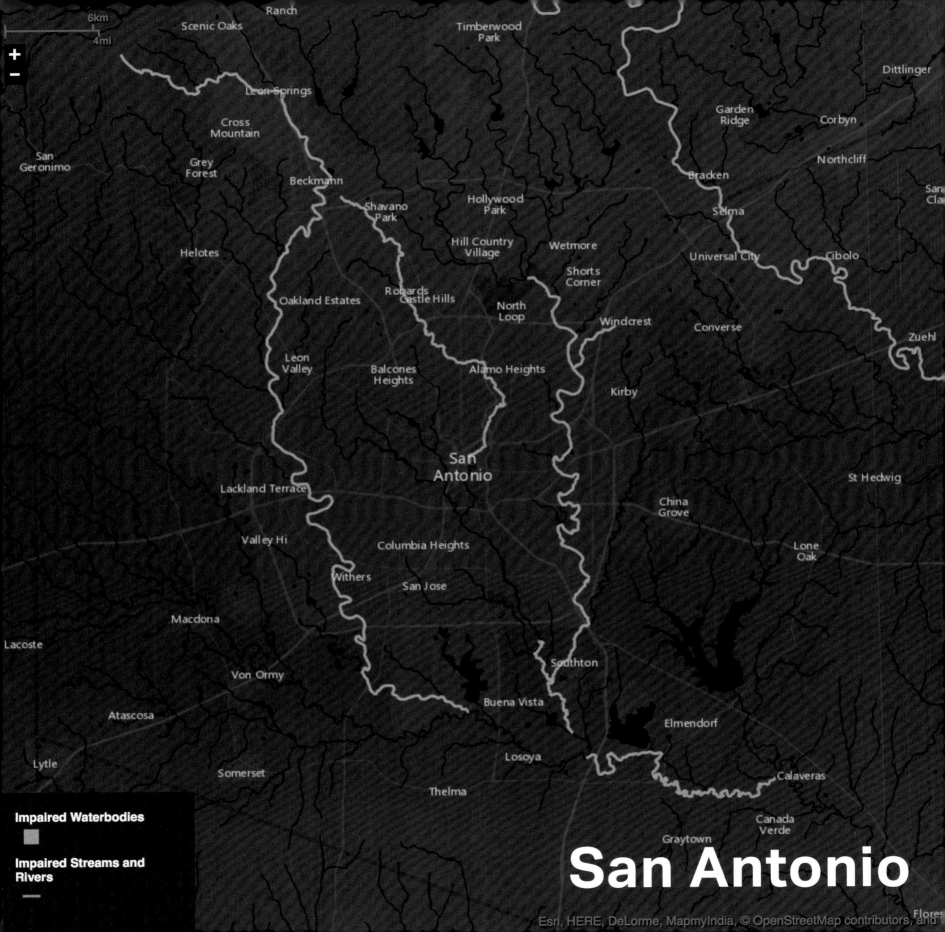

San Antonio

Esri, HERE, DeLorme, MapmyIndia, © OpenStreetMap contributors, and

Impaired Waterbodies

Impaired Streams and
Rivers